Lafka.

Arabic Phrase Book

Arabic translation by
Zohra Inoughi

Phonetic transcription by
Bruce Ingham

Arabic
Phrase Book

Edmund Swinglehurst

HAMLYN
LONDON · NEW YORK · SYDNEY · TORONTO

First published in 1982 by
The Hamlyn Publishing Group Limited
London · New York · Sydney · Toronto
Astronaut House, Feltham, Middlesex, England

© Copyright The Hamlyn Publishing Group Limited 1982

ISBN 0 600 30497 3

Set on Linotype VIP System in Times by Tek Typesetting

Printed in Great Britain by
Hazell Watson & Viney Ltd., Aylesbury, Bucks.

Distributed in the U.S. by
Larousse & Co. Inc., 572 Fifth Avenue, New York,
New York 10036

Contents

Introduction

The Hamlyn Arabic Phrase Book is designed to help the reader who has no previous knowledge of the language. With its aid he should be able to make himself readily understood on all occasions and to cope with the host of minor problems – and some major ones – that can arise when on holiday or travelling in the Middle East and North Africa.

The key to successful speech in a foreign language is pronunciation, and an outline of the principles of vowel and consonant sounds and their usage in Arabic is to be found at the beginning of this book. This is followed by a section dealing with the essential elements of Arabic grammar. A close study of these two sections and constant reference to them will be of the utmost value: with the pattern of sentence construction in mind and a feeling for the sound of the language, the reader will be well equipped to use the phrases in this book.

These are set out in logical order, beginning with the various means of travel and entry to the country. The section on accommodation covers the whole range from hotels and private houses and villas to youth hostels and camping sites. Particular attention is paid in the chapter on eating and drinking to the many varieties of Arabic dishes. Shopping too, is covered in detail: whether the reader wishes to indulge in a shopping spree for local souvenirs or equip the apartment he or she may be using during a prolonged business trip, a selection of appropriate phrases is provided easy to refer to and simple to use.

Entertainment, sightseeing, public services, and general conversations in the hotel are all covered, and there is an important section on looking after your money. In addition to carefully chosen phrases, each section includes an appropriate vocabulary which is as comprehensive as possible, and at the end of the book there are quick-reference metric conversion tables for the more important temperatures, weights and measures and an index to all the phrases.

The Hamlyn Arabic Phrase Book will not only enable the traveller to handle any situation with confidence but will help to make his stay in Arab countries a more enjoyable one.

Guide to Arabic Pronunciation and the Arabic Script

This is intended for people with little or no previous knowledge of Arabic. It is based on English pronunciation and is designed as far as possible to follow the spelling conventions of English, providing an approximate English equivalent for Arabic sounds. All Arabic vowels do, in fact, correspond quite closely to certain English ones. There are, however, some consonants which can be learnt only with the help of an Arabic-speaking person and these are omitted from the Guide. The reader who pays careful attention to this section should be able to follow the phonetic transcription, which is used throughout the book, and thus make himself reasonably well understood in Arabic.

The Vowels

SYMBOL USED IN THE PHONETIC TRANSCRIPTION	APPROXIMATE PRONUNCIATION	EXAMPLE
ā	like *a* in last	nām (he slept)
ee	like *ee* in greet	neel (Nile)
oo	like *oo* in loot	shoof (look)
ai	like *ai* in wait	kwait (Kuwait)
ou	like *ou* in soul	noum (sleep)
a	1 like *a* in sofa or ago	**a**gool (I say)
	2 when stressed, like *u* in cup	**a**na (I) wagt (time)

e	like *e* in met	**weled** (boy)
i	like *i* in lift	**bint** (girl)
u	like *u* in put	**subb** (pour!)

Final Vowels

SYMBOL USED IN THE PHONETIC TRANSCRIPTION	APPROXIMATE PRONUNCIATION	EXAMPLE
y	like *y* in empty	**kitāby** (my book)
o	like *o* in kilo	**nāmo** (they slept)
u	like *ue* in blue	**kitebtu** (you wrote)

Other Vowel Sounds

SYMBOL USED IN THE PHONETIC TRANSCRIPTION	APPROXIMATE PRONUNCIATION	EXAMPLE
eyy	like *ai* in wait with the *y* lengthened	**teyyib** (good)
āy	like *i* in high or *y* in my	**āyila** (family)

The Consonants

SYMBOL USED IN THE PHONETIC TRANSCRIPTION	APPROXIMATE PRONUNCIATION	EXAMPLE
b	like *b* in bat	**bain** (between)
t	like *t* in time	**tis'a** (nine)

th	like *th* in thin	thilth (a third)
j	like *j* in jump	jeeb (bring)
h	like *h* in hat	hāt (bring)
kh	like the Scottish *ch* in loch	khāf (he was afraid)
d	like *d* in dance	**Di**jla (Euphrates)
dh	like *th* in there	dhāk (that)
r	like the rolled Scottish *r*	rās (head)
z	like *z* in zebra	zain (good)
s	like *s* in soul	sār (it became)
sh	like *sh* in shin	shai (thing)
'	like the Cockney pronunciation of *tt* in bottle (bo'le)	sa'ab (difficult)
gh	like the French *r* in rien or like the Scottish *ch* in loch, pronounced with less emphasis	ghair (other)
f	like *f* in four	feeh (there is)
g	like *g* in go	gām (he stood up)
k	like *k* in keen	kān (he was)
ch	like *ch* in change	chelb (dog)
l	like *l* in lamb	lou (if)
m	like *m* in man	min (from)
n	like *n* in none	noor (fire)
w	like *w* in water	wain (where)
y	like *y* in yet	youm (day)

Remember that *r* is always pronounced and is never silent as in English far or car. Similarly the *h* sound must be given its full value, as in **ah**sen (better). Note also that when any consonant is written double, two separate sounds must be produced, i.e. **ket**teb (he dictates) is pronounced rather like cat-tab.

Stress

In Arabic words are generally stressed on the long syllables, e.g. kitāby. If a word contains two long syllables, the one nearer the end of the word bears the main stress, e.g. rejā**jeel**. If a word has no long syllables the stress generally falls on the first syllable, e.g. **wel**ed. In the imitated pronunciation used in this book stress is shown by printing the stressed syllable in bold type:

indek se**ja**yir inglai**zee**ya

In certain phrases, some words of more than one syllable are so lightly stressed that no stress mark is shown in the imitated pronunciation.

The Script

ARABIC LETTER	SYMBOL USED IN THE PHONETIC TRANSCRIPTION	ARABIC LETTER	SYMBOL USED IN THE PHONETIC TRANSCRIPTION
ا	a	ض	dh*
ب	b	ط	t*
ت	t	ظ	dh*
ث	th	ع	‘
ج	j	غ	gh
ح	h*	ف	f
خ	kh	ق	g
د	d	ك	k
ذ	dh	ل	l
ر	r	م	m

ز	z	ن	n
س	s	ه	h
ش	sh	و	w, oo or ou
ص	s*	ى	y, ee or ai

Letters marked with the asterisk * are difficult to describe with reference to English, but are here given their nearest equivalent. There is however a difference in pronunciation between the letters ة and ح, س and ص, ض, ظ and ذ, and ط and ت although they are transcribed ح and ة =h, ص and س =s, and ض, ظ and ذ =dh. Short vowels are not normally represented in the Arabic script, so بن (bn) represents bun (coffee beans). Certain letters have different forms, depending on whether they occur at the end of a word (final) or elsewhere (non-final). The non-final forms are shorter, as can be seen by comparing سم (semm) and مس (mess).

Basic Grammar

Arabic is spoken over a very wide geographical region and has been so for more than 1000 years. There is therefore a considerable variation between the spoken dialects of different areas. In the written form however the difference is slight. Educated people can converse both in their local spoken dialect and in the literary or written form.

This book is designed primarily as a guide to the spoken form of the Arabian Gulf area, but would be useful also in other parts of the Middle East. In general an attempt has been made to give forms which would be acceptable in as wide an area as possible and which would be understood by most Arabic speakers. The grammar dealt with here is limited so as to cover the types of sentences occurring in the phrase book.

The Noun

1. **Number.** In Arabic the noun has three forms: singular, dual and plural. Singular denotes 'one', i.e. **weled** 'a boy', 'one boy', the dual 'two', i.e. weled**ain** 'two boys', and the plural three or more or 'many', as in oul**ād** 'boys', 'some boys'. The form of the dual is the same with all words and has the ending -ain. The plural however differs from word to word, as the following examples show.

weled	'boy'	oulād	'boys'
bint	'girl'	benāt	'girls'
rejjāl	'man'	rejājeel	'men'
seyyāra	'car'	seyyārāt	'cars'
tureeg	'road'	turug	'roads'

2. **Gender.** Nouns in Arabic are either masculine or feminine. The feminine is used for people or things which are biologically feminine such as **mara** 'woman' or **khāla** 'aunt', or for objects which are only linguistically feminine such as am**āra** 'building' or **yed** 'hand'. Feminine nouns in most cases have the ending -a.

3. **Definiteness.** The noun is made definite by adding el- 'the', as in el-weled 'the boy'. The indefinite does not need to be marked in Arabic, so weled means 'boy' or 'a boy'. Similarly oulād means 'boys' or 'some boys'. Adjectives follow the noun in Arabic and agree with it in gender and definiteness, so that when the noun is preceded by el- so is the adjective. 'A good boy' is weled teyyib, 'the good boy' el-weled el-teyyib, and 'the good girl' el-bint el-teyyiba. They also agree with it in number. The demonstratives, the words for 'this', 'that', etc. usually precede the noun in Arabic, but may also follow it. The important ones to learn are:

	MASC	FEM		MASC	FEM
this	hādha	hādhy	that	dhāk	dheek [dheech]
these	hādhoul	hādhouleek [-leech]	those	dhoulāk	dhouleek [-leech]

Remember also that if the demonstratives are used with a noun, the noun must have the article el-: hādha el-rejjāl or el-rejjāl hādha 'this man', hādhoul el-rejājeel 'these men'. If you leave out the word el- 'the', the sentence would mean something else. (See 'to be' and 'to have' in the section on the verb.)

4. **Possession.** In Arabic there is, strictly speaking, no word for 'of'. In order to say 'the man's house' or 'the house of a man' a specific construction is used in which the possessed item precedes the possessor. The definite article el- is placed before the second noun if the phrase is regarded as definite.

bait rejjāl   a man's house *or* the house of a man
bait el-rejjāl   the man's house *or* the house of the man

The word hagg meaning 'property' or 'right' is also used to form an alternative structure meaning something 'like the house belonging to the man', i.e. el-bait hagg el-rejjāl. In other parts of the Arab world different words are used, e.g. māl in Iraq, btā' in Egypt and Syria, and dyāl in North Africa.

In order to express possession of the type 'my house', 'your house', etc. a set of personal pronoun suffixes are used which are added to the noun as in the following examples:

bait	house	**bait**-ha	her house
bait-y	my house	**bait**-na	our house
bait-ek	your (masc. sing.) house	**bait**-kum	your (pl.) house
bait-ich	your (fem. sing.) house	**bait**-hum	their house
bait-a*	his house	**bait**-hin	their (fem.) house

***bait**-u in the western Arabic countries.

If the possessed word is a feminine ending in -a this -a changes to -et before the various suffixes or a possessor noun: seyyāra 'car', seyyārety 'my car', seyyāret khālid 'Khalid's car'.

The word hagg, mentioned above, can also be used to form phrases of the type el-bait hagg-y 'the house belonging to me', 'my house'. Note that these suffixes follow only nouns. If an adjective is involved it does not take the suffix, but must be marked as definite. It follows the noun as also do the demonstratives in these examples:

bint-y el-kibeera	my eldest daughter
weled-y hādha	this son of mine
biyoot-na hādhouleek	these houses of ours

The Verb

The verb in Arabic changes according to the subject or 'actor' and may also do so according to the object or 'recipient' of the action of the verb (known as 'object marking'). The verb has basically four shapes or forms according to whether it is in the present, past, imperative or stative ('denoting a state'). Although these forms differ somewhat for different verb types the prefixes and suffixes are the same. The most common type is exemplified by the verb 'to write' which has the stems -ktib- and kiteb-.

1. PRESENT

ektib	I write	**tekti**been	you (fem. sing.) write
nektib	we write	**tekti**boon	you (masc. pl.) write
yektib	he writes	**yekti**boon	they (masc.) write
tektib	she writes, you (masc. sing.) write		

2. PAST

kiteb	he wrote	**ki**tebna	we wrote
kitebt	I, you (masc. sing.) wrote	**kti**bet	she wrote
kitebty	you (fem. sing.) wrote	**kti**bo	they wrote
kitebtu	you (pl.) wrote		

Note that the 'he' form of the past is the basic form and has no affixes. Other verb types differ only in the shape of stems as can be seen from the following examples.

shāf	he saw	**shā**fet	she saw
shift	I saw	ye**shoof**	he sees
en**ā**dy	I call	nā**dait** ·	I, you (masc. sing.) called
eshidd	I tie	shed**dait**	I, you (masc. sing.) tied
ākil	I eat	**e**kelt	I, you (masc. sing.) ate

3. IMPERATIVE

The imperative is basically the stem with the personal pronoun affixes removed, but showing number and gender marking. Compare the following:

iktib	write!	**ik**tiby	write (fem. sing.)!	**ik**tibu	write (pl.)!
shoof	see!	**shoo**fy	see (fem. sing.)!	**shoo**fu	see (pl.)!
nād	call!	**nā**dy	call (fem. sing.)!	**nā**du	call (pl.)!
shidd	tie!	**shid**dy	tie (fem. sing.)!	**shid**du	tie (pl.)!
ikil	eat!	**i**kly	eat (fem. sing.)!	iklu	eat (pl.)!

4. PARTICIPLE

The participle denotes a state. If the verb is a verb of motion or one which itself denotes a state or the activity of one of the human senses the participle denotes a present state. If the verb is an action verb it denotes a state of completion as in the following examples, where the participle is the second word:

a. Present state:

ana	**mā**shy	I am going
ana	me**sā**fir	I am travelling
ana	jāy	I am coming

ent	sämi'	You are listening
ent	shäyif	You are looking
ent	näyim	You are sleeping

b. State of completion:

ana	kätib	I have written
ana	mit'ashy	I have had dinner
hu	jäyib	he has brought ——
hu	shärib	he has drunk ——
hu	mishtiry	he has bought ——

The participle is also marked for number and gender by the addition of the following suffixes: -a (fem. sing.), -een (masc. pl.), and -ät (fem. pl.). Compare hee **kätib**a 'she has written', hum kät**been** 'they (masc.) have written', and hin kätib**ät** 'they (fem.) have written'.

Other compound tenses can be formed by using the verbs kän 'he was' or **bagha** 'to want'. Some examples of these occur in the phrases. The verb kän 'to be' forms past continuous sentences such as kän **mäsh**y 'he was going', **kän**et **mäsh**ya 'she was going', kint ektib 'I was writing' or 'I used to write' and kint **kä**tib 'I had written'. The verb **bagha** can be used for the future, so eby a**shoof** or eba**shoof** means 'I want to see' or 'I shall see'.

5. OBJECT MARKING

The personal pronoun suffixes mentioned above are also used to mark the object or recipient of the action, as in 'I called *him*' or 'I opened *it*'. These suffixes follow the verb as in the following examples. Note that the suffix for 'me' is -ny.

tishoof-ny	she sees *me*	shäfet-na	she saw *us*
ashoof-ek	I see *you* (masc. sing.)	shäfet-kum	she saw *you* (masc. pl.)
ashoof-ich	I see *you* (fem. sing.)	shäfet-hum	she saw *them* (masc.)
ashoof-a	I see *him*	shäfet-hin	she saw *them* (fem.)
ashoof-ha	I see *her*		

6. 'TO BE' AND 'TO HAVE'

Arabic is somewhat simpler than English as regards the concepts of being and possessing. In a sentence like 'I am an Englishman' or 'I am English', all you need to say is 'I English' (**ana** ing**l**aizy). 'This is good' becomes 'this good' (**hā**dha zain) and 'these are men' 'these men' hā**dhoul** reja**jeel**. Compare the following:

hādha el-rej**jāl**	This man
hādha el-rej**jāl**	This is the man
hādha rej**jāl**	This is a man

Note that the Arabic forms of 'this man' and 'this is the man' are identical.

In the past tense the verb kān 'was' is used in the same way as any other verb: kint fy el-bait 'I was in the house', **kā**net jā**ret**na 'she was our neighbour', kān shābb 'he was young', **kin**na hnāk 'we were there' and **kā**no areb 'they were Arabs'. For the concept 'to have' in Arabic the word 'ind- ('with', 'beside') is used followed by the suffixes, given under 5 above. Thus **ind**-y **ha**jez means 'with me (there is) a reservation' or, as we would say, 'I have a reservation'.

ind-y	I have	**ind**-na	we have
ind-ek	you (masc. sing.) have	**ind**-kum	you (pl.) have
ind-ich	you (fem. sing.) have	**ind**-hum	they (masc.) have
ind-a	he has	**ind**-hin	they (fem.) have
ind-ha	she has		

EXAMPLES:

kān **ind**-hum **ha**jez	They had a reservation (literally, there was with them a reservation)
kān **ind**-y **ha**jez	I had a reservation
dhāk el-rej**jāl** **ind**-a wele**dain**	That man has two sons

7. NEGATION

Sentences are made negative by the use of the particles mā, moo and lā: mā occurs before verbs in such sentences as **mā ki**teb 'He did not write' and **mā** eby 'I do not want'; lā is used for negative wishes or orders: lā **tek**tib 'Do not write', lā **yek**tib 'Let him not write, he had better not write'; moo is used in sentences where there is no verb: **hā**dha moo zain 'This is not good', **ana** moo jou**'ān** 'I am not hungry'. The use of these particles can be learnt more easily by looking at the phrases in the book.

8. THE VERB 'TO WANT'

The Arabic form of this verb differs very much from country to country. The verb **bā**gha/**eby**/**teby**, etc., used in this book, is appropriate to Saudi Arabia and the Gulf countries. In other areas the common forms are as follows: Iraq rād/ye**reed**; Egypt āwiz; Syria, Lebanon and Jordan **biddy/biddek**, etc.; Yemen and Aden **ashty/tishty**, etc.; and North Africa bgha/bgheet, etc. If you are in any doubt the Iraqi verb rād/ye**reed** is the most widely understood as it is the form also used in Classical Arabic.

NOTE. Use of square brackets [ ].

In the Phrase Book square brackets are used in the phonetic transcription to show alternative pronunciations of a particular word or phrase where the written Arabic form remains the same. They are also used where necessary to indicate the pronunciation of alternative translations of words or phrases.

Arabic Spoken

Arabic is spoken throughout the Middle East and in North Africa. There are local dialects in all the Arab countries but the phrases that appear in this book will be understood everywhere.

BAHRAIN is a small emirate on an island in the Arabian Gulf; its total area is 661 sq km (255 sq mi). The wealth from its oil is transforming the country into a modern metropolis surrounded by farmlands made fertile by irrigation projects.

EGYPT, whose history can be traced back to 3000 BC, consists largely of desert through which the Nile creates a fertile strip running from north to south. Cairo, a mixture of modern city and ancient Arab town, lies at the beginning of the Nile delta. Alexandria is situated at its western edge and Port Said is at the entrance to the Suez Canal.

IRAQ stretches from the Arabian Gulf to the borders of Turkey and is watered by the rivers Tigris and Euphrates. Oil has brought great wealth to this country, which was one of the cradles of civilization, and today Baghdad is a modern city of over three million people.

JORDAN is also a desert country except where it borders the river Jordan. Though not one of the oil-producing countries of the Middle East, Jordan has considerable mineral deposits. It is also famous for its archaeological interest, the high spot of which is the city of Petra.

KUWAIT lies at the head of the Arabian Gulf and possesses one of the world's largest oil reserves. The capital city is completely modern and, though surrounded by desert, has an abundance of trees and greenery.

LEBANON, torn by internal strife in recent years, is a beautiful land bordering on the Mediterranean. Beirut is its chief port and capital and other towns whose names echo with historical associations are Tyre, Sidon, Tripoli and Byblos. Archaeological remains are plentiful, especially at Baalbek.

OMAN lies at the south-east corner of the Arabian peninsula. It is an arid and mountainous land but agriculture is carried on along the coast and in the valleys. Oil provides much of the country's revenue. The main cities are Matrah, with a population of 20,000, and Muscat.

QATAR is on a peninsula that juts out into the Arabian Gulf. Its sole resource is oil and the revenue from this has facilitated the building of a modern city at Doha and the development of fruit and vegetable cultivation in a once barren land.

SAUDI ARABIA is the largest Arab country and stretches from the Red Sea to the Arabian Gulf. Its two main cities are Riyadh, the administrative centre, and Mecca, the religious capital. Like other countries rich in oil Saudi Arabia has modernized its cities and developed its social services. The prophet Mohammed was born in Mecca.

SYRIA has a Mediterranean seaboard and its capital is Damascus. In this ancient city there are many fine buildings, including the Great Mosque. Unlike many Arab countries Syria has extensive agriculture which provides enough food for the nation's needs. Oil is one of the main sources of revenue.

THE UNITED ARAB EMIRATES consist of seven sheikhdoms on the Arabian Gulf. Abu Dhabi and Dubai are the largest of these and the richest in oil. Financed by the oil revenue, all the emirates are developing new industries.

YEMEN. There are two Yemeni states, the Yemen Arab Republic, which lies on the Red Sea, and the People's Democratic Republic of Yemen, which faces the Gulf of Aden. Both are mountainous and engage in agriculture and fishing. Aden lies in the People's Democratic Republic.

Algeria, Tunisia, Libya, Morocco and Sudan are also Arabic countries and, though they have much in common with countries of the Middle East, there are also many differences, owing in part to their long association with European culture. It may be found, therefore, that some sections of this phrase book are more appropriate to one Arabic-speaking area than another, and these variations should be borne in mind if apparent discrepancies are encountered.

Here to start with are some simple expressions of greeting and leave-taking:

Good morning.	**sabāh el-khair**	صباح الخير
Good afternoon/ Good evening.	**mesā el-khair**	مساء الخير
Good night.	**tisbah 'ala khair** [**laila sa'eeda**]	تصبح على خير [ليلة سعيدة]
How are you?	**kaif hālek**	كيف حالك؟
I'm very pleased to meet you.	**tesharrafna**	تشرفنا
How do you do?	**ehlen**	اهلا
Goodbye.	**ma' el-selāma** [**bi-emān illāh**]	بأمان الله . [مع السلامة]

Some words of courtesy:

Please.	**min fadhlek** [**tufadhdhal**]	من فضلك [تفضل]
Thank you.	**shukren**	شكرا
It's very kind of you.	**shukren jezeelen**	شكرا جزيلا
You are welcome.	**ehlen wa sehlen** [**merhaba**]	اهلا وسهلا [مرحبا]
Not at all.	**afwen**	عفوا
I am so sorry.	**mite'essif**	متأسف.
Excuse me.	**esefen**	اسفا
It doesn't matter.	**mā yehimm**	ما يهم.

And some questions:

Do you speak English?	**titekellem inglaizy**	هل تتكلم انجليزي
Where is the hotel?	**wain el-findug**	اين الفندق؟
What did you say?	**ish tigool**	ماذا تقول؟

When does the train leave?	**mi**ta **yem**shy el-gi**tār**	متى يمشي القطار؟
Who are you?	min ent	من أنت؟
How much does it cost?	bi**kem hā**dha	بكم هذا؟
How long does it take?	**kem** yākhidh **wagt**	كم يستغرق؟
Which is the road to . . .?	**wain** el-tu**reeg** ila . . .	إين الطريق إلى...؟
Why are we waiting?	**laish** hel inti**dhār**	لماذا الانتظار؟

Finally some useful common phrases:

Yes.	**na'** am [ai] [aiwa] [ai na'am]	نعم.
No.	lā	لا.
Why?	laish [laih]	لماذا؟
How?	kaif [shloun]	كيف؟
When?	**mi**ta [**yem**ta]	متى ؟
What?	ish [wish] [**shi**nu]	ماذا ؟
Where?	wain	اين
How much?	kem [chem]	كم
How many?	**kem wā**hid	كم
Please speak slowly.	te**kell**em ala **meh**lek	تكلم على مهلك من فضلك.
I do not understand Arabic very well.	**mā** efham **ar**eby **zain**	لا أفهم العربية جيدا.
Will you write it down, please?	**ik**tibha min **fadh**lek	اكتبها من فضلك.
How do I say . . .?	**kaif** agool . . .	كيف اقول...؟
What is the meaning of . . .?	ish **ma'**na . . .	ما معنى...؟

Please show me how this works.	rāweeny kaif ya'mel hādha min fadhlek	أرني كيف يعمل هذا من فضلك.
How far is it to . . .?	kem el-mesāfa ila . . . [ish yib'id anna . . .]	كم المسافة إلى...؟
Where is the nearest . . .?	wain [wain egrab . . .] . . .	أين أقرب...؟
What time is it?	el-sā'a kem [el-sā'a baish]	الساعة كم؟
Will you please help me?	mumkin tesā'idny	ممكن تساعدني؟
Can you point to where we are on this map?	mumkin tidelleeny wain hinna ala el-khārita	ممكن تحدد لي أين نحن على الخارطة
Which way do I go?	wain tureegna	أي طريق أتجه؟
Is there an official tourist office here?	feeh mekteb siyāha hina	هل يوجد مكتب سياحة هنا؟
Where is the station/bus stop?	wain el-mehatta/mougif el-bās	أين [المحطة]
Where do I buy the tickets?	min ain nishtery el-tedhākir	من أين نشتري التذاكر؟
We have missed the train.	fātna el-gitār	فاتتا القطار.
Do I turn right/left?	hel nākhidh el-yemeen/el-shimāl	هل اتجه يمين/شمال؟
Do I go straight ahead?	hel emshy mustageem	هل أمشي مستقيم؟
What is the name of this street?	ish ism hādha el-shāri'	ما اسم هذا الشارع؟
How do I get to . . .?	kaif āsil ila . . .	كيف أصل إلى؟
It is too expensive.	hādha ghāly jidden	هذا غال جدا.
Please give me the change.	atny el-bāgy min fadhlek	أعطني الباقي من فضلك.

I am tired.	ana ta'**bān**	.أنا تعبان
I am hungry/thirsty.	ana **jā**yi'/atsh**ān**	أنــا جائع/عطشان
It is very hot/cold.	el-**din**ya harr/**ba**red	الدنيــا حر/برد .
Please take me to my hotel.	wass**il**ny ila el-oo**tail** min **fadh**lek	وصلني إلى الأوتيل من فضلك.
Is the service included?	hel **yesh**mil el-**khid**ma	هل يشمل الخدمة؟
Thank you very much.	**shuk**ren jez**ee**len	شكرا جزيلا

And some idiomatic expressions:

Go away.	imsh [**yal**lah]	إمشي (يالله!)
Leave me alone.	it**rik**ny [**fuk**kny]	اتركني
Shut up.	is**kit**	أسكت
How goes it?	kaif el-ah**wāl**	كيف الأحوال؟
So so.	**ya**'ny	يعني
Don't move.	lā tte**har**rek	لا تتحرك
That's it.	te**mām**	تمام
Carry on.	tu**fadh**dhal [**kem**mil]	تفضل كمل.

All Aboard

The Arabic countries cover a vast area that stretches between the Mediterranean and the Arabian Gulf and along North Africa. This was roughly the extent of the empire set up by the great Muslim expansion following the establishment of Islam by the prophet Mohammed. Today this territory is occupied by many individual states, varying enormously in size and character. Travelling in each country the visitor will find different regulations and different means and standards of travel.

Broadly speaking, most of the travel between Arab countries is best done by air. Railways do exist in some countries such as Egypt, Iraq, Jordan and Lebanon, but the lines are limited and local services poor. Roads, too, are scarce though many of the existing routes are excellent modern highways, thanks to the wealth which oil has brought.

Arrivals and Departures

Going through Passport Control and Customs

Each of the Arab countries has its own requirements for passports and customs procedures and visitors should ensure that they are fully aware of them. English is widely spoken in Arab countries but visitors may sometimes find themselves in areas where only Arabic is understood. It is useful, therefore, to know one or two basic phrases. Apart from making communication easier, they help to establish a friendly relationship with officials and often smooth the passage across frontiers. It should be borne in mind that visitors who have passed through Israel may not be allowed into an Arab country if their passport bears an Israeli entry or exit stamp.

Good morning/good afternoon/good evening.	sabāh el-khair/nehārek sa'eed/mesā el-khair	صباح الخير/نهارك سعيد / مساء الخير.

Here is my passport/ visitor's card.	hādha jewāz sefery/ butāget ziyāra	هـذا جواز سفري / بطاقة زيارة
I am on holiday/ on business.	ana fy ijāza/ indy shughul	أنـا في اجازة/ لشغل
I am visiting relatives/friends.	ana zāyir egārib/asdigā	أنا زائر أقارب / أصدقاء
The visa is on page . . .	el-tesheera ala safhet . . .	التأشيرة على جواز سفري على صفحة...
Here is my vaccination certificate.	hādha shehādet telgeeh	هذه شهادة تلقيح
They did not stamp my passport at the entry port.	mā khatamo ala jewāz sefery ind el-dukhool	لم يختموا جواز سفري عند دخول الميناء.
Will you please stamp my passport? It will be a souvenir of my holiday.	min fadhlek ikhtim jewāz sefery. yekoon tidhkārin li'utlety	من فضلك إختم جواز سفري. سيكون تذكاراً لعطلتي.
I will be staying a few days/two weeks/a month.	ana bāgin kem youm/ isboo'ain/shaher	سأبقى لعدة أيام أسبوعين /شهراً.
I am just passing through.	ana mārrin min hina fagat	انا مار من هنا فقط
My wife and I have a joint passport.	ana wa zoujety lina jewāz sefer wāhid	انا وزوجتي لنا جوازسفر واحد.
The children are on my wife's passport.	el-etfāl fy jewāz sefer zoujety	الأطفال في جواز سفر زوجتي.
I didn't realize it had expired.	mā fahimt inn jewāz sefery intaha	لم أدرك أن جواز سفري قد إنتهى.
Can I telephone the British Consulate?	mumkin ekhābir el-gunsuleeya el-breetāneeya	ممكن أخابر القنصلية البريطانية؟

I have nothing to declare.	mā indy shai edhāhirah	ليس عندي شيء أظاهره.
Do you want me to open my cases? Which one?	tebeeny eftah el-shunat? ai wihda	هل تريد مني فتح حقائبي؟ أي واحدة؟
They are all personal belongings.	killeha aghrādh shakhseeya	كلها أغراض شخصية.
I have a few small gifts for my friends.	indy ba'dh el-hedāya el-sagheera lil-asdigā	عندي بعض الهدايا الصغيرة لأصدقائي.
I have 200 cigarettes.	indy miyatain sijāra	عندي ٢٠٠ سيجارة
They are for my personal consumption.	lil-istihlāk el-shakhsy	للاستهلاك الشخصي
Do I have to pay duty?	lāzim edfa' el-jumruk	هل يجب أن ادفع الجمرك؟
I have no other luggage.	mā indy shunat thānya	ليس عندي حقائب أخرى.
Do you want to see my handbag/briefcase?	teby teshoof hageebety/shuntety	هل تريد أن ترى حقيبة يد/حقيبة شخصية؟
I can't find my keys.	mā elga mefāteehy	لا أجد مفاتيحي.
I have . . . in currency and £100 in traveller's cheques.	indy . . . imla wa miyet jinaih shaikāt siyāheeya	عندي... عملة ومئة جنيه شيكات سياحية
I can't afford to pay duty.	mā egdar edfa' el-jumruk	لا أستطيع أن ادفع الجمرك
Can I leave it here in bond?	mumkin etruk-ha fy el-jumruk	ممكن أتركها في الجمرك؟
Here is a list of the souvenirs I have bought.	hādhy gāyimet el-hedāya elly ishterait-ha	هذه قائمة بالهدايا التي أشتريتها.

You haven't marked my suitcase.	**mā** khetemt ala **shan**tety	لم تختم حقيبتي.
May I leave now?	**mum**kin emshy el-**heen**	ممكن أمشي الآن؟

At Airports, Terminals and Stations

Where can I find	wain elga	أين اجد
a porter?	**ham**mal	الحمـال؟
a luggage trolley?	**trou**ly	ترولي؟
the left luggage office?	**mek**teb el-emā**nāt**	مكتب حفظ الحقائب؟
my registered luggage?	ha**gā**yiby el-mu**sej**jila	حقائبي المسجلة؟
That's my case.	**hā**dhy **shan**tety	تلك حقيبتي.
There's one piece missing.	**dhā**'et **wih**da [nāg**seen** **wih**da]	فقدت حقيبة.
That's not mine.	**hā**dhy mā **heeb** ly	هذه ليست لي.
Have you seen the representative of my travel company?	ent **shā**yif mu**meth**il el-**she**rika el-seeya**hee**ya	هل رأيت ممثل الشركة السياحية؟
Take my bag to the bus/taxi/car.	**ikh**idh **shan**tety ila el-**bās**/el-**tāk**sy/el seyy**ā**ra	خذ شنطتي إلى الباص التكسي/السيارة.
How much per case?	**bik**em el-**shan**ta	كم أجرة الحقيبة؟

Toilets

Where is	wain	أين حمام النساء/
the ladies' toilet/the gentlemen's toilet?	tuw**ā**lait el-nisw**ān**/ tuw**ā**lait el-rij**āl**	حمام الرجال؟

Have you	indek	هل عندك
any soap?	sāboon	صابون؟
any toilet paper?	wareg tuwālait	ورق حمام؟
a towel?	minshefa	منشفة ؟
a comb or hairbrush?	mishut ou firsha	مشط أو فرشاة شعر؟

Telephone

Where are the public telephones?	wain el-tilaifoon el-umoomy	أين التليفون العمومي؟
I need a telephone directory.	eby deleel telaifoon	أريد دليل التليفون.
Where can I get some change?	wain ehassil ala fekka [khirda]	أين أحصل على فكة [صرافة]؟
Can I call this number or do I ask the operator?	mumkin ekhābir mubāshereten ou bwāstet āmil el tilaifoon	ممكن اخابر مباشرة أو بواسطة عامل التليفون؟
May I have Cairo 1234?	eby el-gāhira wāhid ithnain thelātha arbe'a	ممكن القاهرة ١٢٣٤
Can I reverse the charges?	mumkin egeyyid-ha ala . . .? [mumkin yidfa' el-jānib el-thāny]	ممكن اقيدها على...؟
I want a person-to-person call.	eby mukālema shakhseeya	أريد مكالمة شخصية.
I have been cut off.	inguta' el-khatt	إنقطع الخط.
You gave me the wrong number.	ataitny el-ragum ghalat	أعطيتني الرقم الغلط
Is she not in?	mā hy moujooda	أليست موجوده؟
Tell her I called. My name is . . .	gil-leha inny khābart. ismy . . .	خبروها إني تلفنت إسمي...

Taxi Rank

Where can I get a taxi?	wain elga täksy	اين اجد تكسي؟
Please get me a taxi.	min **fadh**lek douwwir-ly täksy	من فضلك شف لي تكسي.
Are you free?	ent **fä**dhy	انت فاضي؟
Take me to El Tahir Square/this address.	ana räyih ila maidän el-tähir/hädha el-'inwän	خذني إلى ميدان الطاهر/ هذا العنوان.
How much will it cost?	kem ykellif [bikem]	كم تكلف الأجرة؟
That's too much.	hädha ketheer jidden	هذا كثير جدا.
Turn right/left at the next corner.	liff ala el-yemeen/el-shimäl ala el-zäwiya el-gädima	در يمين/شمال على الزاوية القادمة.
Go straight on.	imsh mustageem [gubel] [seeda]	امشي مستقيم.
I'll tell you when we arrive.	ana egool-lek idhä wisilna	ساخبرك حين نصل.
Stop!	gif [ougaf]	قـف !
I'm in a hurry.	ana mista'jil	انا مستعجل.
Take it easy!	ala kaifek [ala hounek] [ala mehlek]	على مهلك!
Can you please carry my bags?	mumkin tesheel shunety	ممكن تحمل شنطتي؟

مكتب الحجز.	**mek**teb el-**ha**jez	Booking Office
مكتب وصولات السيارات.	**mek**teb wusoolät el-seyyärät	Cars Check-in Desk

محطة البص.	mehattet el-bās	Coach Station
مصعد.	mis'ad	Escalator
خروج.	khurooj	Exit
مكتب الاستعلامات.	mekteb el-isti'lāmāt	Information Office
مكتب حفظ الحقائب [الأمانات]	mekteb hifdh el-hagāyib [el-emānāt]	Left Luggage
رصيف.	raseef	Platform
حمالون.	hammāleen	Porters
تاكسيات.	tākseeyāt	Taxis
حمام	hammām [tuwālait]	Toilet
غرفة الانتظار.	ghurfet el-intidhār	Waiting Room

Newsstand/Kiosk

Have you got an English paper or magazine?	indekum jereeda ou mejella inglaizeeya	هل عندكم جريدة أو مجلة انجليزية؟
Have you any paperbacks?	indekum kutub rekheesa	هل عندكم كتب رخيصة؟
Which is the local paper?	wain el-jereeda el-mahalleeya	أين الجريدة المحلية؟
Do you sell timetables?	tebee' jedwel muwā'eed	هل تبيع جدول مواعيد؟
Do you sell a guide/map to the city?	tebee' deleel/khārita lil-medeena	هل تبيع دليل/خارطة للمدينة؟
Have you any writing paper? any envelopes? any sellotape? any matches?	indek wareg kitāba dhuroof skouch (Scotch) kibreet [shekhāta]	هل عندك ورق كتابة؟ مظاريف؟ سكوتش؟ كبريت؟

Have you	indek	هل عندك
any stamps	tuwābi'	طوابع؟
a ballpoint pen?	galem	قلم؟
any string?	khait [habel]	حبل؟

Information Bureau

Is there an information bureau here?	feeh **mek**teb isti'lāmāt hina	هل يوجد مكتب إستعلامات هنا؟
Have you any leaflets?	indek neshrāt	هل عندك أي نشرة ؟
Have you a guide to hotels?	indek de**leel** lil-fenādig	هل عندك دليل للفنادق؟
pensions?	bensyou**nāt**	بنسيون؟
youth hostels?	men**ā**zil lil-shebāb	منازل للشباب؟
Do you find accommodation for visitors?	hel tuwaffir el-seken lil-zuwār	هل توفر السكن للزوار
I want a	eby **fin**dig	أريد فندق
first-class/ second class hotel.	**de**reje oola/thānya	درجة أولى ثانية
a pension.	bensyoun	بنسيون
a double room.	ghurfa muzdawija	غرفة مزدوجة
a single room.	ghurfa mufrada	غرفة مفردة
We'll go right away.	nemshy hel-**heen**	سنذهب حالا.
How do I get there?	kaif āsil ila hināk	كيف أصل إلى هناك؟

At Airports

Where is the check-in desk?	wain **mek**teb el-'u**boor**	أين مكتب العبور؟
Can I take this in the cabin?	**mum**kin ākhidh hādhy ila el-tāyira	ممكن آخذ هذه إلى الطائرة؟

Do I have to pay excess?	lāzim edfa' ziyāda	لازم ادفع زيادة؟
You haven't given me a luggage claim tag.	mā ataitny tedhkiret el-'afsh	لم تعطني تذكرة العفش.
I've missed my flight. Can you give me another flight?	fātetny el-tāyira. mumkin ākhidh tāyira thānya	فاتتني الطائرة. ممكن آخذ طائرة أخرى؟
Is there a bar on the other side of the customs barrier?	feeh bār wara sālet el-jumruk	هل هناك بار بعد مغادرة صالة الجمرك؟
Where is the flight indicator?	wain deleel el-rihlāt	أين دليل الرحلات؟
Is there a duty-free shop?	feeh soog hurra	هل هناك سوق حرة؟
Is there another way to go up/down other than by escalator?	feeh tureeg thāny lil-su'ood/lil-nuzool ghair el-mis'ad	هل يوجد طريق آخر للصعود/للنزول غير المصعد؟
Where can I get some flight insurance?	wain yimkin el-husool ala te'meen dhidd el-hawādith el-joweeya	أين يمكن الحصول على تأمين ضد الحوادث الجوية؟
Is there a wheelchair available?	feeh kursy lil-mug'adeen	هل هناك كرسي للمقعدين؟
Is the flight delayed?	hel el-rihla mute'ekhira	هل الرحلة متأخرة؟
At what time do we land?	mita nenzil	متى راح ننزل؟

At Railway Stations

| Where is the ticket office? | wain mekteb el-tedhākir | أين مكتب التذاكر؟ |

One single/return/ first-class/second-class ticket to . . .	**rou**ha bess/**ou**da/ **de**reja **oo**la/**de**reja **thā**nya ila . . .	تذكرة/عودة/ درجة اولى/ تذكرة درجة ثانية إلى...
How much is a child's fare?	**bi**kem el-oulād	بكم تذكرة ولد؟
Can I reserve a seat?/a couchette?	**mum**kin a**ha**jiz **mag**'ad/**koo**shai	ممكن احجز مقعد؟ كوشى
Is there a supplement to pay?	feeh zi**yā**da **thā**nya	هناك أي زيادة ثانية؟
Will there be any food on the train?	feeh **e**kil bil-gi**tār**	ياترى هناك أكل في القطار؟
Do I have to change?	**lā**zim nu**ghey**yir	لازم نغير؟
Which is the platform for the train to Alexandria?	wain ra**seef** el-gi**tār** lil-iskende**ree**ya	اين رصيف القطار للسكندرية؟
At what times does the train leave?	ai **sā**'a **yem**shy el-gi**tār**	أي ساعة يمشي القطار؟

At a Port

Which is quay number six?	wain ra**seef** **sit**ta	اين رصيف ٦؟
From where does the launch leave?	min **ain** yen**ta**lig el-**mer**kab	من اين ينطلق المركب؟
When can I go on board?	**mi**ta **ner**keb	متى نركب؟
Will there be an announcement when visitors must disembark?	hel **yu**'len **mou**'id el-nu**zool** lil-zā**yi**reen	هل سيعلن موعد النزول للزائرين؟
When does the boat leave?	**mi**ta ye**ghā**dir el-**mer**kab	متى تغادر المركب؟

Vocabulary

مقعد	bench	**mag'ad**
سائق الاتوبيس	bus driver	**sāyig bās**
ساعة	clock	**sā'a**
بوابة	gate	**bowwāba**
حارس	guard	**hāris**
مكتب العفش	left luggage office	**mek**teb el-'afsh
خزائن	lockers	**khezāyin**
حمال	porter	**hammāl**
ضابط أمن	security officer	**dhā**bit emn
بوفيه [كفتيريا]	station buffet	**boofai** [kāfetaireeya]
أمر المحطة	station master	**āmer el-mehatta**
سماعة	tannoy	**semmā'a**
محصل	ticket collector	**muhassil**
آلة البيع	vending machine	**ālet el-bai'**
غرفة الانتظار	waiting room	**ghurfet el-intidhār**

En Route

General Expressions

At what time do we start/take off?	mita nebda/nuteer	متى سنبدأ/ سنطير؟
Why is there a delay?	laish el-te'kheer	لماذا التأخير؟
Have I got time to go to the toilet?	indy wagt erooh lil-tuwālait	هل عندي وقت أذهب للحمام؟
I can't find my ticket.	mā elga tedhkirety	لا أجد تذكرتي.
Take my address and passport number.	ikhidh inwāny wa ragum jewāz sefery	خذ عنواني ورقم جواز سفري.
Is this seat reserved?	hādha el-mag'ad mahajooz	هل هذا المقعد محجوز؟

Travelling by Air

Are you the Steward/Stewardess?	ent el-mudheyyif/enty el-mudheyyifa	هل أنت المضيف/ المضيفة؟
Which button do I press to call you?	ai zirr adhrib li-enādeek	أي زر أضرب لأناديك؟
Can you help me to adjust my seat?	mumkin tesā'idny e'addil mag'ady	ممكن تساعدني لأكيف مقعدي؟
Shall I fasten my seat belt?	arbut hizām el-mag'ad	هل أربط حزام المقعد؟
I haven't got a sick bag.	mā indy kees el-ghai	ما عندي كيس الغيء
How high are we flying?	ish irtifā'na el-heen	ما مقدار إرتفاع الطائرة؟
What town is that down there?	hādhy el-medeena ish-ismeha	ما إسم تلك المدينة؟

Is there a map of the route?	indekum khārita lil-tureeg	عندكم خريطة للطريق؟
Are there any duty-free goods available?	indekum bedhāyi' fy el-soog el-hurra	عندكم بضائع في السوق الحرة؟
Can I pay you in foreign currency/in pounds sterling?	mumkin edfa' bil-'umla el-ejnebeeya/ bil-esterleen	ممكن ادفع بالعملة الاجنبية / بجنيهات إسترلنية؟
The airvent is stuck	el-mirwaha 'atlāna	المروحة عطلانة.
May I change my seat?	mumkin egheyyir el-mag'ad	ممكن اغير مقعدي؟

VOCABULARY

aircraft	tāyira	طائرة
air terminal	raseef	رصيف
arrival gate	bāb el-wusool	باب الوصول
ashtray	taffāya	منفضة
flight deck	medrej taiyerān	مدرج طيران
fuselage	haikel el-tāyira	هيكل الطائرة
jet engine	muharrik neffāth	محرك نفاث
light	dhou	ضوء
luggage shelf	reff el-'afsh	رف العفش
propeller	muharrik	محرك
tail	dhail	ذيل
tray meal	seeneeyet el-ekil	صينية الأكل
window	nāfidha	نافذة
wing	jināh	جناح

SIGNS

اربطوا أحزمتكم	urbutu ahzimetkum	Fasten your seat belts
باب الطوارىء	bāb el-tawāry	Emergency exit
ممنوع التدخين.	memnoo' el-tedkheen	No smoking

Travelling by Rail

Is this the train for . . .?	**hādha** gitār . . .	هل هذا قطار...؟
Where is carriage number five?	wain el-**areba** **ragum** **kham**sa	أين العربة رقم خمسة؟
I have a couchette reserved.	**indy** koo**shai** maha**jooz**	عندي كوشي محجوز.
This is my seat reservation.	**hādhy** **tedh**kiret el-**hajez**	هذه تذكرة الحجز.
Is this seat taken?	**hādha** el-**mag**'ad maha**jooz**	هل هذا المقعد محجوز؟
Is the dining car at the front or back?	el-**mat**'am fy **owwel** el-gi**tār** ou **ākhirah**	هل المطعم في أول القطار او آخره؟
Two tickets for the first service, please.	tedhkire**tain** lil-**ga**'da el-**oola** min **fadh**lek	تذكرتين للوجبة الأولى من فضلك
Is the buffet car open throughout the journey?	el-**boofai** mef**tooh** ala **tool** el-**sefera**	هل البوفيه مفتوح على طول؟
Can I leave my big case in the baggage car?	**mum**kin a**hutt** **shan**tety el-ki**beera** fy **arebet** el-'afsh	ممكن أحط الشنطة الكبيرة في عربة العفش؟
Is there an observation car?	feeh **areba** mu**rā**gaba	هل توجد عربة مراقبة؟
What station is this?	ish **hādhy** el-me**hatta**	ما هذه المحطة؟
The heating is on. is off. is too high. is too low.	el-**ted**feeya shag**hāla** mag**foola** she**dee**da dha'**eefa**	التدفئة شغالة . مقفولة . شديدة . ضعيفة .
I can't open/close the window.	**mā** egdar **ef**tah/a**sek**kir el-**nā**fidha	لا أستطيع فتح / إغلاق/ النافذة.

| Where do I have to change? | **wain** a**gheyy**ir | أين لازم أغير؟ |
| Is this where I get my connection for Cairo? | a**gheyy**ir **hi**na lil-**gā**hira | هل أغير هنا للقاهرة؟ |

VOCABULARY

blanket	ba**tā**neeya	بطانية
corridor	me**marr**	ممر
compartment	mag**soo**ra	مقصورة
cushion	wi**sā**da	وسادة
door	**bāb**	باب
luggage rack	**raff** el-'afsh	رف العفش
non-smoking	mem**noo**' el-ted**kheen**	ممنوع التدخين
sleeping berth	se**reer** noum	سرير نوم بقطار
sleeping car	**are**bet noum	عربة نوم

SIGNS

| ممنوع الاطلال من الشباك. | mem**noo**' el-it**lāl** | Do not lean out of the window |
| ممنوع استخدام التواليت أثناء وقوف القطار. | mem**noo**' istikh**dām** el-tu**wā**lait ith**nā** wu**goof** el-gi**tār** | Do not use the toilet while the train is stationary |

Travelling on a Steamer

Where is the purser's office?	**wain mek**teb el-sar**rāf**	أين مكتب الصراف؟
Please will you show me to my cabin?	min **fadh**lek del**liny** ala mag**soo**rety	من فضلك دلني على مقصورتي.
Are you the steward?	ent el-mu**dhey**yif	هل أنت المضيف؟

Is there a children's nursery/shop/ gymnasium?	feeh roudhet atfāl/dukkān/ jimnaizyoom	هل توجد روضة اطفال/ دكان/ جمنيزيم؟
Where can I get some seasick tablets?	wain elga agrās dhidd el-doukha	اين اجد اقراص ضد الدوخة؟
On which side do we disembark?	wain jihet el-nuzool	اين جهة النزول؟
The sea is calm/rough.	el-baher hādy/sākhib	البحر هادي/صاخب
What are those birds? Seagulls?	ish hādhy el-tuyoor nuwāris	ما هذه الطيور؟ نوارس؟
Is there a duty-free shop?	feeh soog hurra	هل يوجد سوق حرة؟

VOCABULARY

aft	muwekhiret el-sefeena	نحو مؤخرة السفينة
anchor	mirsā	مرساة
bridge	burj el-giyāda	برج القيادة (في السفينة)
captain	gabtān el-sefeena	قبطان السفينة
crew	tāgam	طاقم
deck	dhaher el-sefeena	ظهر السفينة
funnel	midkhanet el-sefeena	مدخنة السفينة
lifebelt	hizām el-nejāt	حزام النجاة
lifeboat	gārib el-nejāt	قارب النجاة
mast	sāry	صاري
officer	dhābut	ضابط
port (harbour)	meena	ميناء
port (left)	yisār el-sefeena	يسار السفينة
radar	rādār	الرادار
raft	remth toufa	رمث طوفة
rail	soor	سور
starboard	maimenet el-sefeena	ميمنة السفينة

Signs

خطر	**kha**tar	Danger

Travelling by Coach

Is this the coach for Beirut?	**hād**ha el-bās **rā**yih ila bai**root**	هل هذا الباص إلى بيروت؟
Can I sit near the driver?	**mum**kin ag'id yemm el-**sā**yig	ممكن أجلس جنب السائق؟
Are the seats numbered?	el-me**gā**'id mu**rag**gama	هل المقاعد مرقمة؟
Do I pay on the coach?	**ed**fa' el-si'r **ba**'ad mā **er**kab	هل أدفع في الباص؟
Does it stop often?	**yā**gaf fy ma**kā**nāt ket**hee**ra	هل يقف كثيراً؟
Would you mind closing the window? It's draughty.	**mum**kin ti**sek**kir el-shib**bāk**. el-**ho**wa gowy	ممكن تسكر الشباك؟ الهواء قوي.
Can you help me to carry my luggage?	**mum**kin tisā'**id**ny fy haml el-**shun**at	ممكن تساعدني في حمل الشنط؟

Vocabulary

back seat	**mag**'ad **khal**fy	مقعد خلفي
driver	**sā**yig	السائق
foot rest	**jin**āh	جناح
front seat	**mag**'ad e**mā**my	مقعد أمامي
guide	**mur**shid	مرشد
luggage compartment	mag**soo**ret el-'afsh	مقصورة العفش.

Buses

Where is the bus stop?	**wain** me**hat**tet el-bās	أين محطة الباص؟
Does one have to queue?	lāzim **nel**zim el-sira	لازم نصف على الدور؟
Do I need a queue ticket?	lāzim **ākh**idh **tedh**kiret el-dour	لازم نحصل على تذكرة الدور؟
Can I buy a book of tickets?	**mum**kin **esh**tery **def**ter tedhākir	ممكن أشتري دفتر تذاكر؟
Do you go by the Abbasid Palace?	te**murr** min yemm gasr el-'abbāseeya	هل تمر من طريق قصر العباسية؟
Will you tell me when we reach the El Tahrir Bridge?	**mum**kin tikh**bir**ny **lem**men **nā**sil ila jisr el-tah**reer**	ممكن تخبرني لما نصل جسر التحرير؟
I want to get off at the next stop.	e**ben**zil bilme**hat**ta el-**gā**dima	أريد أنزل المحطة القادمة
Will you ring the bell please?	**mum**kin **tadh**rib el-**ja**res min **fadh**lek	ممكن تضرب الجرس من فضلك؟
I want to go to King Hussein Street.	e**ba**rooh ila **shā**ri' el-**me**lik hu**sain**	أريد أن أذهب شارع الملك حسين.
When is the first bus/next bus/last bus?	**mi**ta by**i**jy **ow**wel bās/el-bās el-**thā**ny/el-bās el-**ā**khir	متى يجي أول باص/ التاني/ الآخر.

موقف الباص.	**mou**gif el-bās	Bus stop

Other Vehicles

Where can I hire	**wain** este'jir	أين أستأجر
a bicycle?	derrāja	دراجة ؟
a moped?	derrāja bimu**h**arrik sa**gh**eer	دراجة بمحرك صغير؟
a tricycle?	derrāja bithelā**th** ajlāt	دراجة بثلاث عجلات؟
a tandem?	derrāja bimag'a**dain**	دراجة بمقعدين؟
Please put some air in this tyre.	**mum**kin **tin**fukh **h**ādha el-'ajel	ممكن تنفخ هذا العجل؟
One of the spokes is broken.	**wā**hid min shu'ār el-derrāja meksoor	أحد شعار الدارجة مكسور.
The brake is not working.	el braik at**lā**n [ta'**bā**n]	البريك عطلان
Do you have a bicycle with gears?	**in**dek derrāja bi**gair**	عندك دراجة بجير؟
The saddle needs lowering/raising.	el-**mag**'ad yeby ten**zeel**/**rafe**'	المقعد محتاج تنزيل/رفع.
Are there any horse-drawn vehicles at this resort?	feeh areb**ā**t khail **h**ina	هل توجد عربيات خيل هنا؟
Will you put the roof down, please?	**mum**kin tine**zz**il el-**gh**ata min **fadh**lek	ممكن تنزل الغطاء من فضلك؟
Will you take the children on the driver's box?	**mum**kin t**ā**khidh el-atf**ā**l yemm el-s**ā**yig	ممكن تأخذ الأطفال جنب السائق؟

bicycle pump	min**fā**kh el-derrāja	منفاخ الدراجة
carrier	**gafas**	قفص
chain	**sil**sila	سلسلة

crossbar	āridha	عارضة
donkey	himār	حمار
handlebars	migwed	مقود
harness	tagum	طقم
lamp	lemba	لبة
mudguard	refref	رفرف
pedal	bedāl	بدال
rear light	el-noor el-khalfy	النور الخلفي
whip	kerbāj [shillāgh]	كرباج

Walking About

IN TOWN

Is this the main shopping street?	hādha el-soog el-re'eesy	هل هذا السوق الرئيسي؟
Where is the	wain	أين
town hall?	el-beledeeya	قاعة الاحتفالات؟
police station?	merkez el-shurta	مركز الشرطة؟
tourist office?	mekteb el-seeyāha	مكتب السياحة؟
In what part of town are	fy ai gism min el-medeena	في أي مكان من المدينة تقع
the theatres/ nightclubs?	el-mesārih/ el-melāhy	المسارح / الملاهي الليلية؟
Can I get there by bus/on foot?	mumkin āsil hināk bil-bās/meshy	ممكن أصل هناك بالباص/مشي؟
Where is the nearest station?	wain egrab mehatta	أين أقرب محطة؟
Where is the nearest bus stop/taxi rank?	wain egrab mougif bās/garāj tāksiyāt	أين أقرب موقف باص/كراج التكسيات؟
Is there a market in the town?	feeh soog fil-beled	هل يوجد سوق في البلد؟

Is the business centre near?	el-**mer**kez el-ti**jā**ry ge**reeb**	هل المركز التجاري قريب؟
Must one cross at the traffic lights?	**lā**zim **na**'ber min me**marr** el-mu**shāt**	هل لازم نعبر من ممر المشاة؟
Do pedestrians have right of way here?	mes**mooh** lil-mu**shāt** el-'u**boor** min **hi**na	هل مسموح للمشاة العبور من هنا؟
Is there a public toilet near?	feeh tu**wā**lait u**moo**my ge**reeb**	هل يوجد مرحاض عمومي قريب؟

VOCABULARY

castle	**ga**sur	القصر
cathedral	kātaid**rāl**	الكاتدرائية
cemetery	**meg**bera	مقبرة
church	ke**nee**sa	الكنيسة
city centre	wast el-me**dee**na	وسط المدينة
concert hall	**gā**'et el-moo**see**ga	قاعة الموسيقى
courts	me**hā**kim	محاكم
docks	**mee**na	أرصفة الميناء
exhibition	**ma**'radh	المعرض
factory	**mas**na'	المصنع
fortress	**ga**sur [**gel**'a]	الحصن
fountain	nā**foo**ra	النافورة
gardens	he**dā**yig	الحدائق
government buildings	me**bā**ny el-hukoo**mee**ya	المباني الحكومية
harbour	**mee**na	الميناء
lake	bu**hai**ra	البحيرة
monastery	dair	الدير
monument	nusb tidh**kā**ry	النصب التذكاري
mosque	**jā**mi'	الجامع
museum	**met**-haf	المتحف
old town	me**dee**na ge**dee**ma [el-**deer**a]	المدينة القديمة
opera house	dār el-**ou**bera	دار الأوبرا
palace	**ga**sur [be**lāt**]	القصر

park	hedeega [muntezeh]	الحديقة
pyramids	ahrām	الأهرام
ruins	āthār	الآثار
shopping centre	merkez tijāry	المركز التجاري
stadium	estādyoom	الاستاد
statue	timthāl	التمثال
stock exchange	boorsa	البورصة
subway	nefag	نفق
traffic lights	ishārāt el-muroor	إشارات المرور
tower	burj	البرج
university	jāmi'a	الجامعة
zoo	hadeeget el-haiwān	حديقة الحيوان

IN THE COUNTRY

May we walk through here?	mumkin nedkhul min hina	ممكن ندخل من هنا؟
Is this a public footpath?	hādha tureeg 'ām	هل هذا طريق للجمهور؟
Is fishing forbidden?	said el-simek memnoo'	هل صيد السمك ممنوع؟
Which way is north/south/ east/west?	wain el-shimāl/el-jinoob/ el-sherg/el-gherb	أين الشمال/الجنوب/ الشرق/الغرب؟
Is there a bridge across this stream?	feeh jisr li'uboor hādha el-naher	هل يوجد جسر لعبور هذا الجدول؟
How far is the nearest village?	ish tib'id anna egrab gerya	كم تبعد أقرب قرية؟
I am lost. Can you please direct me to . . .?	ana tāyih. mumkin tidelleeny ala . . .	أنا ضايع . ممكن تدلني على...؟
Will you please show me the route on this map?	mumkin tidelleeny el-tureeg ala el-khārita	ممكن تدلني الطريق على الخارطة؟

Vocabulary

barn	**mekh**zen ghi**lāl**	مخزن غلال
bird	tair	طير
canal	ge**nāt**	قناة
cliff	**hā**fet el-**ji**bel	حافة الجبل
	[**shi**fet el-**ji**bel]	
cow	ba**ge**ra [**hā**yisha]	بقرة
desert	**bā**diya [berr] [sah**rā**]	صحراء
dog	kelb [chelb]	كلب
farm	**mez**ra'a	مزرعة
field	hakl [**mez**ra'a]	حقل
footpath	**sik**ka [**da**reb]	سكة
forest	**ghā**ba	غابة٠
hill	tell [**ji**bel] [mer**gāb**]	تل
horse	hu**sān** [**fa**res, *pl.* khail]	حصان
goat	**mi**'za (*pl.* **ma**'az)	معزة
inn (coffee house)	**fin**dug [ge**ha**wa]	استراحة
lake	bu**hai**ra	بحيرة
marsh	hour (*pl.* ah**wār**)	مستنقع
mountain	**ji**bel (*pl.* ji**bāl**)	جبل
olives	zai**toon**	زيتون
orchard	bis**tān**	بستان
peak	**gum**ma	قمة
pond	**bir**ka [**bir**cha]	بركة
pool	ghe**deer**	غدير
river	**ne**har [shatt]	نهر
sea	**ba**her	بحر
sheep	kha**roof** (*pl.* **ghe**nem)	خروف
spring	beer [**bir**ka] [**bir**cha]	نبع
stream	**ne**har	تيار
swamp	hour (*pl.* ah**wār**)	مستنقع
tree	she**je**ra	شجرة
valley	**wā**dy [she'**eeb**]	وادي [شعيب]
village	**ger**ya [**fe**reeg] [**dee**ra]	قرية
vineyard	**ke**rem 'ineb	كرم عنب

waterfall	shellāl	شلال
well	beer [birka] [bircha]	بئر
wood	ghāba	غابة

Motoring

At the Frontier

Here is my	hādha	هذا
registration book.	sened el-tesjeel	سند التسجيل
insurance certificate.	bouleeset el-te'meen	بوليصة التأمين
driving licence.	rukhset el-suwāga	رخصة السواقة
I have an international licence.	indy rukhsa douleeya	عندي رخصة دولية.
This is a translation of my British licence.	hādhy terjuma li-rukhsety el-breetāneeya	هذه ترجمة لرخصتي البريطانية.
This is a hired car. Here are the documents.	hādhy seyyāret eejār. hādhy el-ourāg	هذه السيارة بدون سائق. هذه الأوراق
Do you want to open the boot?	teby tiftah el-sendoog	هل تريد فتح الطبون؟
I arrived today.	wisilt el-youm	وصلت اليوم.
I am staying for two weeks.	ana bāgin isboo'ain	سأبقى أسبوعين.
We are passing through on the way to . . .	hinna fy tureegna ila . . .	نحن في طريقنا إلى....
Does this customs post close at night?	merkez el-jemārik hādha m'azzil bil-lail	هل نقطة الجمرك هذه تغلق ليلا؟
When?	mita [ai wagt]	متى ؟
Do you want me to stop the engine?	tebeeny etaffy el-muharrik	هل تريد مني إطفاء المحرك؟

On the Road

The road system in Arabic countries varies considerably from one country to another. In those bordering the Mediterranean the network is more developed. Usually the roads around the cities are good and often the big cities are connected by highways, but otherwise in general the road networks are inadequate and petrol stations scarce outside the towns.

Can you tell me the way to Tangier?	**wain** el-tureeg ila **tan**ja	أين الطريق إلى طنجة؟
How many kilometres is it?	**kem** keeloumiter	كم كيلومتر ؟
Is it a good road?	el-tureeg zain	هل الطريق صالح؟
Is it hilly/flat/straight/ winding?	el-tureeg bil-jibāl/munbasut/ mustageem/mite'arrij	هل الطريق جبلي/منبسط/ مستقيم/ متعرج؟
What is the speed limit on this section?	ish el-sur'a el-guswa ala hādha el-tureeg	ما هي السرعة القصوى على هذا الطريق؟
Will you point out the route on this map, please?	**mum**kin terāweeny el-tureeg ala el-khārita	ممكن ترينا الطريق على الخريطة؟
How much does this section of road cost?	**kem** yikellif el-muroor ala hādha el-tureeg	كم يكلف المرور على هذا الطريق؟
Do I pay at the exit?	**lāzim edfa'** ind el-khurooj	لازم أدفع عند الخروج؟
I am sorry, I have no change.	mite'essif mā indy **fekka** [khirda]	متأسف، ما عندي فكة.
How far is it to the next petrol station?	ish yib'id anna egrab mehattet bānzain	ما المسافة إلى أقرب محطة بنزين؟
I want twenty-five litres, please.	eby khemsa wa ashreen liter min fadhlek	أريد ٢٥ لتر، من فضلك.
Give me . . . worth.	atny bi . . .	أعطني بـ ...

Fill her up, please.	abbeeha min **fadh**lek	إملأها من فضلك.
Please check the oil and water.	min **fadh**lek ik**shif** ala el-zait wa el-māy	من فضلك إكشف على الزيت والماء.
Can you please put some air in the tyres?	el-tāyer**ā**t yib**ghā**leha **how**a	انفخ لي العجلات من فضلك.
Could you top up the windscreen fluid?	**mum**kin te'**abb**y māy el-mess**āh**āt	ممكن تملأ ماء للمساحات؟
Have you any water for the battery?	**in**dek māy lil-bat**ā**reeya	هل عندك ماء للبطارية ؟
Please clean the windscreen.	min **fadh**lek **nadh**if el-jām el-em**ā**my	من فضلك نظف الزجاج الأمامي.
Have you any towels?	**in**dek **war**eg [**min**shefa] [**wus**la]	هل عندك منشفة؟
Have you got a car wash?	**in**dek mu**ghess**il el-seyy**ā**rāt	هل عندكم مغسلة السيارات؟
Do you sell yellow filters for the headlights?	te**bee'** mus**fā**t **suf**ra lil-dhou el-em**ā**my	هل تبيع مصفاة صفراء للضوء الأمامي؟
Can I park here?	**mum**kin e**wagg**if **hi**na	ممكن أركن هنا؟
Where is the nearest car park?	**wain** feeh **mou**gif lil-seyy**ā**rāt	أين أقرب موقف للسيارات؟

Trouble with the Police

Usually the police are polite and helpful to visitors, but they are more likely to be so if you appear friendly and co-operative. A few phrases in their language can sometimes work miracles.

I'm sorry, I did not see you signal.	**af**wen mā shift el-ish**ā**ra	متأسف لم أر الاشارة.
I thought I had right of way.	fak**kart** hakk el-u**boor** lee	فكرت أن لي حق لعبور.

I apologize. I won't do it again.	mā esawwy kidha ba'ad ebeden	متأسف لن أفعل ذلك مرة ثانية.
Here is my name and address.	hādha ismy wa inwāny	هذا إسمي وعنواني.
This is my passport.	hādha jewāz sefery	هذا جواز سفري.
Do I have to pay a fine?	lāzim edfa' gherāma	لازم أدفع غرامة؟
How much?	kem [ishged]	كم؟
I haven't got any cash on me. Can I settle up at the police station?	mā indy mesāry. mumkin edfa' fy dāyiret el-shurta	ما معي مصاري. ممكن أدفع في دائرة الشرطة؟
Thank you for your courtesy.	shukren. alla yhafudhek	شكرا على ذوقك.

Car Rental

I want to hire	eby este'jir	أريد إستئجار
a small car.	seyyāra sugheera	سيارة صغيرة
a saloon car.	seyyāra sāloun	سيارة صلون.
a large car.	seyyāra kebeera	سيارة كبيرة.
a sports car.	seyyāra isbour	سيارة سبور.
a van.	wanait	كاب.
I shall need it for ten days.	ebeeha asheret aiyām	أريدها عشرة أيام.
How much is the daily charge?	kem el-ujra bil-youm	كم الأجرة في اليوم؟
Is it cheaper by the week?	bil-isboo' erkhas	بالأسبوع أرخص؟
Does that include everything?	hādha yeshmel kill shai	هل هذا يشمل كل شيء؟
What is the mileage charge?	kem yikellif el-meel	كم يكلف الميل؟

Does the insurance cover the car and the passengers?	el-te'**meen yesh**mel el-seyyāra wa el-ru**kkāb**	هل التأمين يشمل السيارة والركاب؟
Where do I pick up the car?	**wain** estelim el-seyyāra	اين أحصل على السيارة؟
Can you bring it to my hotel?	**mum**kin te**jeeb**ha ila el-**fin**dug	ممكن تحضرها إلى الفندق؟
Can I leave it at another town or at the airport?	**mum**kin etruk-ha fy medeena **thān**ya ou bil-ma**tār**	ممكن اتركها في مدينة اخرى او في المطار؟
Is there a deposit to pay?	**lā**zim edfa' are**boon**	لازم أدفع عربون؟
Do you accept cheques?	**mum**kin tākhid**hoon** shai**kāt**	ممكن تأخذوا شيكات؟
Will you please check the documents with me?	khel-ne**shoof** el-ou**rāg** ana wa **ent** je**mee'**	من فضلك راجع أوراقي.
Will you show me the gears and the instrument panel?	min **fadh**lek **rā**weeny el-gair wa **lou**het el-te**hakk**um	من فضلك ادیني الجیر ولوحة التحكم.
Is the tank full?	khe**zān** el-we**good** mu'**abba**	هل خزان الوقود معبأ؟

Road Signs

اشعل النور الأمامي	ish'al el-noor el-e**māmy**	Switch on your headlights
منطقة عمل أمامك	**man**tiget **a**mel e**māmek**	Roadworks ahead
الطريق محفر	el-tu**reeg** mu**haffer**	Damaged road surface
إحذر الحجارت	i**hdher** el-hi**jārāt**	Falling stones
جمرك	**jum**ruk	Customs

التجاوز غير ممنوع	el-te**jā**wuz ghair mem**noo'**	End of no overtaking
ممنوع التجاوز.	mem**noo'** el-te**jā**wuz	No overtaking
ممنوع مرور المشاة/والشاحنات	mem**noo'** mu**roor** el-mu**shāt**/el-**shāhināt**	No pedestrians/heavy vehicles
حفر.	**hu**fer	Pot holes
مزلقان	mez**leghān**	Level crossing
اسبقية المرور للسيارات على الطريق الرئيسي.	esbag**hee**yet el-mu**roor** lil-seyy**ārāt** el-**gā**dima ala el-tu**reeg** el-re'**eesy**	Priority for vehicles on main road
الأسبقية للسيارات القادمة من اليمين.	esbag**hee**yet el-mu**roor** lil-seyy**ārāt** el-**gā**dima min el-ye**meen**	Priority for vehicles coming from the right
عبور مشاة.	u**boor** mu**shāt**	Pedestrians only
تحويل.	taha**weel**	Diversion
طريق ضيق/منزلق	tu**reeg dheyy**ig/**mun**zelig	Narrow/slippery road
ممنوع الدخول	mem**noo'** el-du**khool**	No entry
حافظ على اليمين.	il**zem jā**nib el-ye**meen**	Keep to the right
مكان إنتظار	ma**kān** intid**hār**	Parking permitted
ممنوع الانتظار.	mem**noo'** el-intid**hār**	Parking prohibited
منحني عالي ٣ كيلومتر	mun**han**iya ala the**lāth keelou**miter	Bends for 3 kilometres

Trouble on the Road

OTHER PEOPLE'S

There has been an accident five kilometres back.	sār **hā**dith ala bu'd **khams keelou**miter	وقع حادث على بعد خمس كيلومتر

Will you phone the police, please?	min **fadh**lek **ut**lub el-**boulees** [el-**shur**ta]	من فضلك أطلب البوليس.
No, I did not see it happen.	la **mā** shift el-**hā**dith	لا ، لم أشاهد الحادث.
The car's registration number was . . .	**ra**gum el-**sey**yāra . . .	لوحة رقم السيارة...
I do not think anyone is hurt.	e**dhunn mā** u**seeb ah**ed	أظن لم يصب أحد.
Someone is badly hurt	u**seeb wā**hid biju**rooh** she**dee**da	أصيب واحد بجروح بالغة.

Yours

Are you all right?	ent bi**khair**	أنت بخير؟
My passengers are not hurt.	**mā** u**seeb ah**ed min **jemā**'ety	لم يصب أحد من ركابي.
The car is damaged.	el-**sey**yāra mas**doo**ma	السيارة انكسرت
May I have your insurance details?	**at**ny **wa**reget el-te'**meen** min **fadh**lek	أعطني بوليصة التأمين من فضلك.
Your name and address, please?	el-**ism** wa el-in**wān** min **fadh**lek	الاسم والعنوان ، من فضلك؟
Will you please fill out this form?	**ab**by **hā**dhy el-isti**mā**ra min **fadh**lek	إملأ هذه الاستمارة من فضلك؟
I think we shall have to call the police.	e**dhunn lā**zim **nat**lub el-**boulees**	أظن لازم نطلب البوليس.
Excuse me, would you mind being a witness?	**yim**kin te**koon shā**hid	هل يمكن تكون شاهد؟
It happened because he braked suddenly.	**ha**deth **kid**ha li'**enn**ehu **fer**mel **faj**'a	حدث هذا لأنه فرمل فجأة.

He came out of a side road without signalling.	jā min shāri' far'y bidoon ishāra	أتى من شارع فرعي بدون إشارة.
He tried to overtake on a narrow stretch of road.	hāwel yitejāwiz fy mukān dheyyig	حاول ان يتخطى في مكان ضيق.
He turned off without signalling.	in'ataf bidoon ishāra	أنعطف بدون إشارة.
May I explain to someone who understands English?	mumkin eshrah lihadin yitekellem inglaizy	ممكن أشرح لأحد يتكلم إنجليزي؟

If you are unfortunate enough to have an accident, be sure to get all the details from the other driver involved. Your insurance company will have provided you with an accident report form. Fill it up on the spot with the help of the other driver. Above all, keep cool.

Breakdown

If you have a breakdown put the red triangle behind your car at once or you may be penalized. Get the car off the road if possible.

Thank you for stopping. I am in trouble.	alla yahafudhek indy mushkila	شكرا على توقفك . عندي مشكلة.
Will you help me?	mumkin tisā'idny	ممكن تساعدني؟
My car has broken down.	ta'attilet seyyārety	تعطلت سيارتي؟
I have locked myself out of the car.	gafelt el-seyyāra wel-mefāteeh dākhil	قفلت السيارة والمفاتيح بداخلها.
Will you tell the next garage or breakdown service vehicle that you pass?	min fadhlek ikhbir gerāj ou islāh seyyārāt fy tureegek	من فضلك أخبر أقرب جراج أو إصلاح السيارات في طريقك.

Will you please telephone a garage for me?	min **fadh**lek ut**lub**-ly ge**rāj**	من فضلك اطلب لي جراج.
Can you give me a lift to the next telephone?	**mum**kin tuwassilny ila tilai**foon**	ممكن توصلني إلى اقرب تليفون؟
Can you send a breakdown truck?	**mum**kin tidouw**wir**-ly seyy**ā**ret winsh	ممكن تبعث سيارة ونش؟
I am three kilometres from Tripoli.	ana ala bu'd te**lā**thet keelou**miter** min tu**rā**bulus	انا على بعد ثلاثة كيلومتر من طرابلس.
Will you be long?	tite'**ekhir**	هل تتأخر؟
There's something wrong with the engine.	el-mo**tour** feeh **atal**	الموتور عطلان.
The clutch is slipping.	el-ke**lāch yin**zelig	الكلتش ينزلق.
There is a noise from the . . .	el-seyy**āra bi**ha sout fy el-	السيارة بها صوت في......
The brakes are not working.	el-fe**rāmil bi**ha **atal**	الفرامل عطلانة.
The cooling system is leaking.	muw**āseer** el-m**āy** makh**roo**ma	مواسير الماء مخرومة.
My fan belt is broken.	sair el-**mir**waha mek**soor**	سير المروحة مكسور.
I've got a flat tyre.	el-**tā**yir kher**bān** [mef**shoo**sha]	العجلة منفشة.
Would you please mend this tyre?	min **fadh**lek **sal**lih h**ā**dhy el-**tā**yir	من فضلك اصلح هذه العجلة.
The electrical system has failed.	**kah**ruba el-seyy**āra fee**ha **atal**	كهرباء السيارة عطلانه.
The engine is overheating.	el-mo**tour hā**my **jid**den	الموتور حامي جدا.
The car won't start.	el-seyy**āra mā** te**door**	السيارة لا تدور.

What is the matter?	ish el-**mush**kila	ما المشكلة؟
Is it	hiya	
broken?	meksoora	مكسورة؟
burnt out?	maharooga	محروقة؟
disconnected?	ghair muwassila	غير موصلة؟
jammed?	ghalat bil-touseel	غلط بالتوصيل؟
Is it leaking?	yekhurr [yeherrib māy]	هل يخر؟
Is there a short circuit?	feeha mās kahrubāyee	هل به ماس كهربائي؟
Does it need a new part?	yeby git'a ghiyār	هل تحتاج قطعة غيار؟
Is there a Ford agent in town?	feeh wikālet ford fil-medeena	هل توجد وكالة فورد في المدينة؟
Can you send for spare parts?	**mum**kin tehassil ala gita' ghiyār	ممكن تحصل على قطع الغيار؟
Is it serious?	el-**a**tal kebeer	هل العطل كبير؟
How long will it take to repair?	**mi**ta **yim**kin islāh-ha	متى يمكن إصلاحها؟
Can I hire another car?	**mum**kin este'jir seyyāra **thān**ya	ممكن استأجر سيارة أخرى؟
What will it cost?	kem yikellif [bikem]	كم تكلف؟ [بكم]
I will get the part flown from Britain.	ejeeb gita' el-ghiyār min breetānya	سأحصل على قطع الغيار من بريطانية.
Your mechanic has been very kind. I would like to tip him.	el-mekāneek lateef **jid**den. eba'**teeh** bakhsheesh	كان الميكانيكي لطيفا جدا. أريد أن أعطيه بقشيش.

Vocabulary

battery	batāreeya	البطارية
brake lining	tail el-ferāmil	الفرامل
brakes	ferāmil	تيل الفرامل

bulbs	lembāt kahrubāeeya	لمبات كهربائية
carburettor	kārburātair	الكاربراتير
clutch	klāch	الكلتش
cooling system	jihāz el-tebreed	جهاز التبريد
dipstick	silk fahus el-zait	سلك فحص الزيت
distributor	distribeetoor	الدستربيتور
dynamo	deenāmou	الدينامو
electrical system	kahrubā el-seyyāra	كهرباء السيارة
engine	motour	الموتور
exhaust pipe	ādim	العادم
fan	mirwaha	المروحة
filter	filter	الفلتر
fuel pump	tulumbet el-benzeen	طلمبة البنزين
fuel tank	khizān el-benzeen	خزان البنزين
gears	teroos [gairāt]	التروس
generator	deenāmou	الدينامو
handbrake	hāndbraik	هاندبريك
headlights	noor el-emāmy	النور الأمامي
heating system	jihāz el-tedfiya	جهاز التدفئة
horn	herin	آلة التنبيه (زامور)
ignition	teshgheel	تشغيل
indicator	ishāra	الاشارة
lubrication system	tezyeet	تزييت
radiator	rādyātair	الرادياتير
reflector	'ākis	العاكس
seat	mag'ad	مقعد
silencer	māsooret el-'ādim	ماسورة العادم
sparking plug	boojiya	بوجية
speedometer	addād el-sur'a	عداد السرعة
suspension	springāt	السوستة
transmission	amood el-kerdān	عمود الكردان
wheels	ajelāt	العجلات
windscreen wipers	messāhāt	المساحات

A Place to Stay

Except in those Arab countries where tourism has been an established industry for some time, the accommodation available is usually the equivalent of European four- and three-star hotels. In some of the smaller states such as Qatar or Oman there are only three or four hotels altogether. Where a hotel industry exists, the classification is usually on a star or class basis and it is under the direction of the Ministry or Bureau of Tourism.

Cheap accommodation in hostels or camp sites may be found in countries such as Algeria, Egypt and Morocco.

Hotels and Pensions

Finding a Room

I am travelling with the . . . travel agency	ana mesāfir ma' **mek**teb el-siyāha . . .	انا مسافر مع مكتب السياحة...
Here is my hotel coupon.	hādhy **tedh**kiret **fin**dugy	هذه تذكرة فندقي.
My room is reserved.	el-**ghur**fa maha**jooza**	الغرفة محجوزة.
I am travelling independently.	ana mesāfir liwahady	انا مسافر لوحدي.
Will a porter bring my luggage in?	**yim**kin el-bow**wāb** yi**dakh**khil el-shunat	هل يمكن الحمال يدخل الحقائب؟
Can I leave my car here?	**mum**kin e**khall**y el-seyyāra **hi**na	ممكن أترك السيارة هنا؟
Is there a car park?	feeh **mou**gif seyyā**rāt**	هل يوجد موقف سيارات؟
Are you the receptionist/ concierge/manager?	ent mu**wadh**if el-istig**bāl** el-bouw**wāb**/el-mu**deer**	هل انت موظف الاستقبال/ البواب/ المدير؟

Have you	indek	هل عندك
a single room/double room?	ghurfa mufreda/ghurfa muzdouwija	غرفة مفردة/ غرفة مجوز
a three-bedded room?	ghurfa li-theláthet eshkhás	غرفة لثلاثة أشخاص؟
a room with twin beds?	ghurfa bi-sereerain	غرفة بسريرين؟
a room with a bath and separate toilet?	ghurfa bi-hamám u tuwálait	غرفة بحمام وتواليت منفصل؟
a room with bath or shower?	ghurfa bi hamám ou doush	غرفة بحمام او دوش؟
a room with a balcony?	ghurfa leha balkônai	غرفة لها بلكونة؟
a room looking over the front/back?	ghurfa mushrifa/fy el-khalf	غرفة مشرفة/ في الخلف؟
How much is it per day/per week?	kem ujret-ha fy el-youm/fy el-isboo‘	كم أجرتها في اليوم/في الاسبوع؟
Is there a reduction for a longer stay/for children?	feeh takhfeedh lil-igáma el-toweela/ lil-atfál	هل يوجد تخفيض للاقامة الطويلة /للأطفال؟
Are there special mealtimes for children?	feeh ougát mu‘ayyena lik-ekil mshán el-atfál	هل توجد أوقات معينة لوجبات الأطفال؟
I don't want to pay more than . . . per day.	má eby edfa‘ ekther min . . . youmiyyen	لا أريد ان ادفع اكثر من... يوميا.
Have you anything cheaper?	má indek shai erkhas	هل عندك شيء أرخص؟
Do I have to fill in a visitor's card?	lázim e‘abby butáget ziyára	لازم أملاء بطاقة زيارة؟
Here is my passport.	hádha jewáz sefery	هذا بسبوري.
When will you return it?	mita terajji‘ha	متى ترجمه؟
I'd like to go up to my room right away.	eby atla‘ ila ghurfety hel-heen	أريد ان اطلع إلى غرفتي فورا.

Will you send up the luggage?	mumkin tuweddy el-shunat foug	ممكن تطلع الحقائب فوق؟
This case is for room 3 and that one is for number 12.	hādhy el-shanta lil-ghurfa thelātha u hādheek li-thenā'sher	هذه الحقيبة لغرفة رقم ٣ وتلك لرقم ١٢.
May I have the room key?	mumkin te'ateeny miftāh el-ghurfa	ممكن تعطيني مفتاح الغرفة؟
Is the key in the door?	el-miftāh fy el-bāb	هل المفتاح في الباب؟
Where is the lift?	wain el-mis'ad	أين المصعد؟
Do I work it myself?	emeshsheeh ana	هل أستعمله لنفسي؟
Do you do breakfast?	tisowwy el-futoor	هل تحضر الفطور؟
Do you do lunch?	tisowwy el-ghada	هل تحضر الغداء؟
Can you put all extras on my bill?	mumkin tehutt el-ziyādāt ala hisāby	ممكن تحط أي زيادة عل حسابي؟
Is there a post box in the hotel?	feeh sendoog bereed bil-findug	هل يوجد صندوق بريد بالفندق؟
Can you get the daily papers for me?	mumkin tijeeb-ly el-jerāyid el-youmeeya	ممكن تحضر لي الجرائد اليومية؟

Moving In

This room is too small/large/noisy/ dark/high up.	hādhy el-ghurfa sugheera jidden/ kebeera/dousha/ dhalma/āliya	هذه الغرفة صغيرة جدا/كبيرة دوشة/ظلمة/ عالية.
Haven't you got a double bed?	mā indek sereer li-shakhsain	هل عندك سرير مجوز؟
Please make the twin beds into one double.	mumkin tegarrib el-sereerain li-ba'adh	ممكن تقرب السريرين لبعض؟
I need a child's cot.	eby mehed lil-tufil	أريد سرير للطفل.

I shall need	eby	احتاج
another pillow.	wisāda **thā**nya	وسادة ثانية
another blanket.	butāna **thā**nya	بطانية ثانية.
some clothes · hangers.	allāgāt lil-melābis	علاقات للملابس
some writing paper.	wareg lil-kitāba	ورق للكتابة.

| The bedside light is not working. | el-dhou bi**jā**nib el-fi**rā**sh feeh **a**tal | الضوء بجانب الفراش عطلان. |

| The bulb is broken. | el-**lem**ba mek**soo**ra | اللمبة مكسورة. |

| Which is the hot/cold tap? | **wain** hane**fee**yet ' el-māy el-**sā**khin/ el-māy el-**bā**rid | أين حنفية الماء الساخن/ الماء البارد؟ |

| Is this the electric razor socket? | **hā**dha sou**kait** me**kee**net el-hi**lā**ga | هل هذا الكبس لماكينة الحلاقة الكهربائية؟ |

| What is the voltage? | **kem** foult | كم فولت؟ |

| This plug doesn't fit. | **hā**dha el-blek ghair mu**nā**sib | هذا البلك غير مناسب. |

| Have you got an adaptor? | **in**dek mu**how**wil | هل عندك محول؟ |

| Is there an electrician in the village? | feeh kaharu**bā**ee fy el-**ger**ya | هل يوجد كهربائي في القرية؟ |

| Is there a hotel laundry? | feeh **magh**sela bil-**fin**dug | هل توجد مغسلة بالفندق؟ |

| Are there facilities for washing and ironing clothes? | **yim**kin **ghu**sel wa **kow**y el-me**lā**bis | هل يمكن غسل وكي الملابس؟ |

| The blind is stuck. | si**tā**ret el-shib**bā**k **feeh**a **a**tal | ستارة النافذة عطلانة. |

| Will you bring me a bottle of drinking water? | min **fadh**lek jeeb-ly māy lil-**shur**eb | من فضلك احضرلي زجاجة ماء للشرب. |

Can I leave valuables in the hotel safe?	**mum**kin e**khally** ba'adh el-**esh**ya fy el-khi**zā**na	ممكن اترك أشياء قيمة في خزانة الفندق؟
What time is \ breakfast/lunch/ dinner?	**mi**ta wagt el-fu**toor**/el-**gha**da/ el-'asha	متى موعد الفطور/ الغداء/ العشاء؟
Could we have breakfast in our room?	**mum**kin **nā**khidh el-fu**toor** fy ghur**fet**na	هل يمكن نتناول الفطور في غرفتنا؟
Does the hotel do packed lunches?	el-**fin**dug ye**had**hir sānd**wee**shāt	هل يحضر الفندق ساندوتشات؟

Small Hotels and Pensions

Do you have set times for meals?	feeh ou**gāt** mu'eyyina lil-ekil	هل لكم أوقات معينة للأكل؟
May I have a towel and soap?	min **fadh**lek **atny min**shefa wa sā**boon**	من فضلك اعطني منشفة وصابون؟
At what time do you lock the door at night?	**mi**ta ti**sek**kir el-**bāb** bil-**lail**	متى تغلق الباب في الليل؟
May I have a key?	**mum**kin te'a**teeny** mif**tāh**	ممكن تعطيني مفتاح؟
Can I leave the car in the street?	**mum**kin e**khally** el-sey**yāra** bil-**shāri'**	ممكن اترك السيارة في الشارع؟
Will our things be safe?	agh**rādh**na e**mee**na	هل أغراضنا في أمان؟
Where is the nearest garage?	**wain** feeh ge**rāj grey**yib	أين أقرب جراج؟

Paying the Bill

| May I have my bill please? | eby el-hi**sāb** min **fadh**lek | أريد الحساب من فضلك؟ |
| Will you prepare my bill for first thing tomorrow? | **mum**kin te'a**teeny** el-hi**sāb ouw**wel shee **buk**ra | ممكن تحضر فاتورتي قبل كل شيء غدا؟ |

I think there is a mistake.	**edhunn** feeh **ghalat**	أعتقد هنا غلط.
I don't understand this.	**ma**ni **fā**him **hā**dha	لا أفهم هذا.
May I pay by cheque?	**mum**kin **ed**fa' shaik	ممكن أدفع شيك؟
Yes, I have a Eurocheque card.	**na'am in**dy **kārt** benk	نعم ، عندي كارت بنك.
Do you accept credit cards?	hel **teg**bal **kārt** raseed **masrefy**	هل تقبل كارت رصيد مصرفي؟
Is service included?	el-**khid**ma mahasooba	هل الخدمة محسوبة؟
Is VAT included?	el-**dhareeba** mahasooba	هل الضريبة محسوبة؟
I would like a receipt, please.	eby el-**wa**sal min **fadh**lek	أريد الوصل من فضلك.
Please forward my mail to . . .	min **fadh**lek **how**wil re**sā**yily ila . . .	من فضلك حول رسائلي إلى...
We have enjoyed ourselves very much.	is**tā**nesna ke**theer**	لقد قضينا وقتا طيبا جدا.
May I have a leaflet?	**mum**kin **ā**khidh **nesh**ra	ممكن أخذ نشرة؟

VOCABULARY

bar	**bār**	بار
barman	**boy**	ساقي
bed	se**reer** [**tekhet**]	سرير
chair	**kur**sy	كرسي
chambermaid	**khā**dima	خادمة
children's playground	ha**dee**get el-atfāl	حديقة الأطفال
discotheque	**mar**gas [**deesko**]	مرقص
door	**bāb**	باب
hall	**sā**la [**gā'a**]	قاعة
lift	**mis**'ad	مصعد
light switch	**mif**tāh el-dhou	مفتاح الكهرباء
lounge	**ghur**fet je**loos**	غرفة جلوس

luggage porter	hamm**ā**l	حمال
manager	mu**deer**	مدير
mirror	mr**ā**ya	مراة
night club	mel**ha** laily	ملهى ليلي
playroom	g**ā**'et el-**li**'ib	قاعة اللعب
radio	r**ā**dyo	راديو
restaurant	mat'am	مطعم
stairs	**da**rej [**si**llem]	درجات [سلم]
swimming pool	**mes**bah	حمام السباحة
telephone operator	**ā**mil el-telai**foun**	عامل التليفون
waiter	ger**soon**	جرسون
waitress	ger**soo**na	جرسونة
wardrobe	khiz**ā**net mel**ā**bis	خزانة ملابس
window	shib**bā**k	شباك

Catering for Yourself

Villas and Apartments

I have booked a villa/an apartment.	ha**jezt** **fee**la/**sheg**ga	حجزت فيلا/ شقة.
Here is my voucher.	h**ā**dhy **tedh**kiret el-**ha**jez	هذه تذكرة الحجز
Will you please show me around?	**mum**kin ter**ā**weeny el-bait	ممكن تفرجني على البيت؟
Where is the light switch/ power point/fuse box?	**wain** **mif**t**ā**h el-dhou/el-kubs/ sen**doog** el-**fyooz**	اين السويتش / الكبس / صندوق الفيوز؟
Do all the outside doors lock?	hel yu**sek**ker kill el-ebw**ā**b el-kh**ā**ri**jee**ya	هل كل الأبواب الخارجية تغلق؟
How do the shutters work?	kaif **ya**'mel el-der**rā**f	كيف يعمل الدراف؟

Please show me the hot water system.	min **fadh**lek **rā**weeny jihāz tes**kheen** el-māy	من فضلك أرينـي جهاز تسخين الماء.
Where is the mains valve?	**wain** sammām el-enābeeb	أين صمام الأنابيب؟
Are gas cylinders delivered?	hel yejee**boon** silind**rāt** el-ghāz	هل توصلوا أسطوانات الغاز؟
At what time does the house help come?	**mi**ta tijy el-**khā**dima	متى تأتي الخادمة؟
Can we have three sets of house keys?	**mum**kin te'a**teeny** the**lath** tagum lil-mefāteeh	ممكن تعطينا ثلاثة نسخ لمفاتيح البيت؟ .
When is the rubbish collected?	**mi**ta yejma'**oon** el-zi**bā**la	متى تجمع الزبالة.
Are the shops near by?	el-soog **grey**yib	هل السوق قريب من هنا؟
Where is the bus stop/station?	**wain** me**hat**tet el-bā**sāt**/ **mou**gif el-bā**sāt**	أين محطة الأوتوبيس/ موقف الأوتوبيس؟
Have you a map of the resort?	**in**dek **khā**rita lil-**man**tiga	هل عندك خريطة المنطقة؟

Camping

There are few camp sites in the Middle East. It is important to check with the tourist office before setting off.

Where can we camp for the night?	**wain nig**der ni**khey**yim hel-**lai**la	أين نستطيع أن نعسكر الليلة؟
Is there a site free?	feeh makān **khā**ly	هل يوجد مكان خال؟
Do you rent out bungalows? tents? cooking equipment?	**yum**kin este'**jir** bange**lai khai**ma me'ad**dāt** el-**ta**bukh	هل يمكن إستئجار بنكلة؟ خيمة؟ معدات الطبخ؟

Are there	feeh	هـل
toilet and washing facilities?	tuwālait wa makān lil-ghasil	يوجد حمام ومكان للغسل؟
cooking facilities?	yumkin el-tabukh	هل يمكن الطبخ؟
How much does it cost per night?	bikem el-laila	بكم الليلة؟
Can I put my tent here?	mumkin ehutt el-khaima hina	ممكن أحط الخيمة هنا؟
Is there room for a trailer?	feeh makān lil-trailer	هل يوجد مكان للتريلة؟
Is there a night guard?	feeh hāris el-lail	هل يوجد حارس ليلي؟
Where is	wain	أين
the camp shop?	el-dukkān	دكان المعسكر؟
the restaurant?	el-mat'am	المطعم
the nearest shopping centre?	egrab soog	أقرب سوق؟
At what time do we have to vacate the site?	mita lāzim neghādir el-makān	متى لازم نترك المعسكر؟
Where is the drinking water tap?	wain hanefeeyet māy el-shureb	أين حنفية الشرب؟

VOCABULARY

barbecue	showy [kebāb]	شوى
basin	maghsila [houdh]	حوض
bucket	satil	جردل
camping gas	butagāz	غاز تخييم
grill	showwāya	شواية
guy ropes	ahabāl el-khaima	حبل لشد الخيمة
ice bucket	jerdel el-thelj	جردل الثلج
insecticide	mubeed el-hasherāt	مبيد الحشرات
knife	sikkeen [sicheen]	سكين
mosquito repellent	tārid el-hasherāt	طارد للحشرات

sleeping bag	**fer**sha sefe**ree**ya	فرشة سفرية
spade	**mis**-ha	مسحاة
stove	**fi**ren	فرن
tent	**khai**ma (*pl.*, khi**yām**)	خيمة
tent peg	**wa**ted **khai**ma	وتد خيمة
waterproof sheet	**sher**shef dhidd el-**māy**	شرشف ضد الماء

Youth Hostelling

Is there a youth hostel in this town?	feeh bait lil-she**bāb** fy **hā**dhy el-me**dee**na	هل يوجد بيت للشباب في هذه المدينة؟
Have you room for tonight?	**in**dekum ma**kān** el-**lai**la	هل عندكم مكان الليلة؟
We are members of the Youth Hostels Association.	**hin**na a'**dhā** jem**'ee**yet b**yoot** el-she**bāb**	نحن أعضاء جمعية بيوت الشباب.
What are the house rules?	ish gu**wā**neen el-bait	ما هي قوانين البيت؟
How long can we stay?	**kem** youm **nig**dar **nib**ga	كم يوم نستطيع أن نقيم؟
Is there a youth hostel at . . .?	feeh bait she**bāb** fy . . .	هل يوجد بيت شباب في...

Eating and Drinking

Strict Muslims do not drink alcohol and in some countries, such as Saudi Arabia, even visitors are not allowed alcoholic drinks. In others drinks can be obtained only in tourist hotels. Most Arabs will take tea, coffee, milk or mineral drinks with their meals or on other social occasions.

Arab food is usually copious and delicately spiced and the main ingredients are lamb or mutton and fish. Hotels in Arab countries usually include Arab specialities but the basis of their menus is European.

Most restaurants frequented by visitors to Arab countries are of the starred variety but in many of the countries there are humbler eating places which will provide the same meals as those eaten by the local people. In these one may often see Arab families, or parties celebrating a special occasion, and a meal follows a certain set of rules. Pork is not eaten nor are dishes including the blood of the animal and cooking with wine is, strictly speaking, not allowed.

A traditional meal begins with the passing of a bowl of water in which the guests dip their fingers. Next several dishes are served up as hors d'oeuvres before the main dish, which usually consists of mutton and rice. The meal is eaten with the hands and the host will often pass his guest some of the choice pieces from the large central dish on which the food is placed. The serving of coffee is a signal that the meal is at an end.

Please recommend a restaurant which is	min **fadh**lek ig**t**arih **mat**'am	من فضلك اقترح مطعما
good.	zain	جيدا.
not too expensive.	lā ykoon **ghā**lya	ليس غاليا جدا.
typical of the region.	mi**thā**ly bil**man**tiga	مثالي بالمنطقة.
where there is music.	feeh moo**see**ga	فيه موسيقى.
a four-star establishment.	**dare**ja **oo**la	مؤسسة درجة أولى.
A Chinese/Indian/Arab/Italian/French restaurant.	**seen**y/**hin**dy/**ar**eby/ee**tā**ly/**faren**sy	صيني/هندي/عربي/ايطالي/فرنسي.

Is there a good snack bar nearby?	feeh kafee**tair**ya **zai**na **grey**yib	هل يوجد سناك بار جيد قريب؟
Where can I find a self-service restaurant?	**wain** el**ga mat**'am self ser**fees**	أين أجد مطعم سلف سرفيس؟
Do I need to reserve a table?	**lā**zim eha**jiz** maiz	هل لازم أحجز طاولة؟
I'd like a table for two	min **fadh**lek eby maiz li-nefa**rain**	من فضلك أريد طاولة لشخصين
at nine o'clock, please.	lil-**sā**'a **tis**'a	الساعة ٩.
away from the door.	be'**ee**da an el-**bāb**	بعيدة عن الباب.
in the corner.	min'**azi**la	منعزلة.
away from the kitchen.	be'**ee**da an el-**mat**bakh	بعيدة عن المطبخ.

At the Restaurant

The Arab equivalent of saying grace:		
before food.	bis**millah**	بسم الله
after food.	al-**hamd** lil**lāh**	الحمد لله
A table for four, please.	maiz mshān **arbe**'a min **fadh**lek	طاولة لـ ٤ ، من فضلك.
Is this our table?	**hā**dha el-maiz **lī**na	هل هذه طاولتنا؟
This table will do fine.	**hā**dha el-maiz zain	هذه الطاولة تناسبنا.
The tablecloth is dirty.	el-**suf**ra **wes**kha	مفرش السفرة وسخ.
The table is unsteady.	el-maiz ma**hoob thā**bit	الطاولة مخلخلة.
The ashtray is missing.	**mā** feeh taf**fā**ya	طفاية السجاير مفقودة.
May I see the menu?	**mum**kin e**shoof** el-**men**yu	مكن أرى قائمة الاكل؟
We will have an aperitif while we look at it.	nte**nāw**el aberi**teef bain**-ma ne**shoof** el-**men**yu	سناخذ بعض الشراب بينما نرى قائمة الاكل.

Please bring the wine list.	min **fadh**lek jeeb gāyimet el-ne**beedh**	من فضلك أحضر لنا قائمة النبيذ.
Have you a set menu?	in**dek**um **wej**bet el-**youm**	هل عندكم وجبة؟
What do you recommend today?	ish-tu**was**sy el-youm	ماذا تقترح اليوم؟
What does it consist of?	**wish**-hee [**shin**-hee]	ما هي المكونات؟
It sounds good. I'll try it.	**chin**nah zain. ana ā**khidha**	أظن هذا عظيم. سأخذه.
The soup is cold. Warm it up, please.	el-**shour**ba bārida. **sakh**inha min **fadh**lek	الشوربة باردة. سخنها. من فضلك.
This fork is not clean. May I have a clean one?	**hādh**y el-**shou**ka ma heeb nu**dhee**fa. **at**ny **shou**ka nu**dhee**fa	هذه الشوكة ليست نظيفة. من فضلك أعطيني شوكة نظيفة؟
Please call the waiter.	min **fadh**lek **ut**lub el-gar**soon**	من فضلك أطلب الجرسون.
We did not order this.	mā **ta**labna **hādh**a	لم نطلب هذا.
I'd like to speak to the head waiter.	**eby** e**kell**im el-**ra**ees min **fadh**lek	أريد أن اتكلم مع المتر من فضلك.
It's very good.	a**dheem** [mum**tāz**]	عظيم.
Have you any house wine?	in**dek**um ne**beedh** khās bil-**mat**'am	هل عندكم نبيذ خاص بالمطعم؟
I'd like a half bottle/a carafe.	**eby** nusf ze**jā**ja/**dou**rag min **fadh**lek	أريد نصف زجاجة/ دورق. من فضلك.
Which is the local wine?	**eyy**ehin el-ne**beedh** el-me**hall**y	أي من النبيذ محلي؟
The children will share a portion.	el-at**fāl** yāk**loon** ma'na	ياكلون الأطفال معنا.
May we have some water?	**jeeb**-lina māy min **fadh**lek	من فضلك أحضر لنا ماء.

Have you any mineral water?	**in**dekum miyāh ma'a**den**eeya	هل عندكم مياه معدنية؟
Have you a special chair for the child?	**in**dekum **mag**'ad khās lil-**tu**fil	هل عندكم مقعد خاص للطفل؟
Please bring some cushions.	min **fadh**lek **jeeb**-lina mekhad**dāt**	من فضلك احضر لنا مخدات.
Where are the toilets?	**wain** el-ham**mām**	اين الحمام؟
May I please have the bill?	el-hi**sāb** min **fadh**lek	الحساب من فضلك؟
Is the service included?	hel **yesh**mil el-**khid**ma	هل يشمل الخدمة

VOCABULARY

bill	hi**sāb**	الحساب
cheese	**jib**na	جبنة
dessert	**hil**wa	حلوى
fish	**sim**ek [**sim**ech]	سمك
fork	**shou**ka [**ching**āl]	شوكه
fruit	fa**wā**kih [**mai**wa]	فواكه
glass	ku**bā**ya [glās]	كباية
knife	sik**kee**na [si**chee**na]	سكينة
meat	**la**hem	لحم
menu	**gāy**met el-**ek**il [**men**yu]	قائمة الاكل
mineral water	mi**yāh** ma'a**den**eeya	مياه معدنية
napkin	**fou**ta	فوطة
oil	zait	زيت
salad	sa**lā**ta	سلطة
salt	**mi**leh	ملح
soft drink	a**seer**	عصير
soup	**shour**ba	شوربة
spoon	**mal**'aga [**ghā**shooga]	ملعقة
starter	**mez**za [**our**dovr]	مزة
sweet	**hil**wa [**des**ert]	حلوى
table	maiz [**tāw**la]	طاولة

vegetables	khudhrawāt	خضروات
vinegar	khall	خل
wine	nebeedh [sherāb] [khamur]	نبيذ
wine list	gāyimet el-nebeedh	قائمة النبيذ

The Menu

In most conventional restaurants in Arab countries the menu will be international, containing many French and Italian dishes. In the tourist countries the menu will often be exhibited outside the restaurant, though this is not always the case.

There are many specialized restaurants in Arab countries. For example, some specialize in charcoal grilled lamb, others in fish and shellfish. In addition there are snackbars, fruit juice bars and pastry shops.

Meals are usually eaten late: lunch from 13.00 to 15.00 and dinner from 20.00 to 23.00 hours.

Starters

Starters are usually called Mezze in all Arab countries and consist of similar kinds of food, ranging from nuts, olives, chick peas and cheeses to salads and more complicated items such as stuffed vine leaves or egg dishes. Mezze are always small dishes designed to whet the appetite for the main meal to follow.

باب غنوج	baba ghanoosh	aubergine with tahina
بورك	boorek	savoury flaky pastry
سلطة خيار باللبن	salāta khiyar liben	cucumber and yoghourt
فتوش	fattoosh	Syrian bread salad
فول نابت	fool nābit	puree of dried white beans
حنود شامي	hanood shāmy	garlic and ground rice salad

حمص	**hum**mus	chick pea paste
كفتة فراخ	**kuf**ret fer**ākh**	fried chicken balls
سلطة خضار مشكل	sal**ā**tet **khud**her mishe**kkel**	mixed salad
سلطة مشوية	sal**ā**ta meshwee**ya**	Tunisian fish salad
طحينة بالسمك	ta**hee**na bil-simak	fish with tahina
طحينة	ta**hee**na	a paste made with sesame meal
تبولة	tab**boo**la	cracked wheat salad
ورق عنب	wareg **in**eb	stuffed vine leaves

Soups

بيض بالليمون	baidh bil-lai**moon**	chicken consommé with beaten egg and lemon
فتة	feta	Egyptian lamb soup
شورية فول نابت	**shour**bet fool **nā**bit	white bean soup
حامض	**hā**mudh	chicken and vegetable soup with lemon
ملوخية	meloo**khee**ya	Egyptian green melokhia leaf soup
شورية سمك	**shour**bet simek	fish soup
شورية فراخ	**shour**bet fir**ā**kh	chicken soup
شورية خضار	**shour**bet **khud**har	vegetable soup

Fish

Most Arab countries have plentiful fish and these include well-known European varieties. River fish, too, are found in the Tigris and Euphrates and in minor rivers in North Africa. Nile fish are usually rather muddy in flavour.

أصابع سمك	es**ā**bi' **sim**ek	fish sticks
سمك طرطور	simek tar**tour**	fish with garlic sauce
سمك مقلي	simek **mag**ly	fried fish
سمك مشوي	simek **mesh**wy	grilled fish
صيادية	seyy**ā**dee**ya**	fish rice

Meat

شوا	shu**wa**	steamed lamb Moroccan style
كوس كس	koos**koos**	a North African dish consisting of lamb stew served with semolina
دفينة	de**fee**na	an Egyptian stew with chick peas and beans
كفته بالرز	**kuf**ta bil-ruzz	minced meat with rice
كفتة مشوية	**kuf**ta mesh**wee**ya	minced meat sausages done on a skewer
كفتة مبرومة	**kuf**ta mab**roo**ma	minced meat with pine nuts
خروف محشي	khar**oof mah**shy	roast lamb on a spit
لسان العصفور	li**sān** el-as**four**	lamb stew with fine pasta (literally 'birds' tongues')
لحم بالكرز	**lah**ma bil-**kar**ez	meat balls with cherries
مزاة	mu**zāt**	shin of veal stew
قوزي	**gouz**y	roast kid on a spit
كباب باللبن	ke**bāb** bil-**li**ben	kebab with yoghourt

Poultry

بط	batt	duck
قدرة فراخ	**gid**ret fe**rākh**	a Moroccan chicken stew
فريك	fe**reek**	Egyptian chicken with wheat and hard-boiled eggs
حمام مشوي	ham**mām mesh**wy	grilled pigeons
كفتة فراخ	**kuf**tet fe**rākh**	chicken balls
طاجن طفاية	**tā**jin tu**fā**ya	a Moroccan dish of boiled saffron chicken

Vegetables

In Arab countries the vegetable dish is given special attention. It is prepared in a number of different ways, often as a dish on its own and not merely as the accompaniment to meat.

بامية	**bāmiya**	okra or ladies' fingers
كوسة بجينة	**koo**sa bi **ji**bna	marrow with cheese
ليمون مكبوس	lai**moon** mak**boos**	pickled lemons
طرطوفة	tar**too**fa	Jersualem artichokes
طرشي لفت	**tur**shi left	pickled turnips
رز بدفين	ruz bi de**feen**	rice with meat and chick peas

Desserts

قطايف	**gu**tāyif	pancakes in syrup
بلوزة	be**loo**za	a kind of mousse with almonds and pine nuts
بسبوسة باللبن الزيادي	bas**bou**sa bil **li**ban za**bā**dy	semolina mould with yoghourt
بقلاوة	bak**lā**wa	thin pastry with nuts
قشطة	**gish**ta	clotted cream
كنافة	ku**nā**fa	fine strands of pastry held together with syrup and nuts
معمول	ma**'amool**	stuffed tartlets
سنبوسك باللوز	sem**boo**sa bil-louz	almond rolls

Drinks

Islam forbids the drinking of alcohol and this rule is applied rigorously in some countries, such as Saudi Arabia, though in others drinking is permitted in moderation. Beer is brewed in Egypt, Lebanon and Jordan, where it is a popular drink. Wine production is increasing and local wines will be found on restaurant menus. These have romantic names such as Omar Khayam, Ptolemy, and Queen Cleopatra. Imported wines are also available.

Soft drinks are widespread and many Arab receptions serve only these. Fresh fruit juice is abundant and delicious thanks to the variety of fruit available. Fruit juice bars and pavement stands will squeeze out the juice of fruit specially for individual customers.

Among the fruit (and vegetable) juices which are usually available are:

جزر	**ji**zer	carrot
عنب	in**eb**	grape
ليمون	lai**moon**	lemon
مانجة	**mān**ja [**amba**]	mango
برتقال	burte**gāl**	orange
رمان	rum**mān**	pomegranate
تمرهندي	**temur hin**dy	tamarind

Coffee is also widely drunk on social occasions. The coffee is usually prepared in the Turkish fashion and can be taken with or without sugar. Shopkeepers and businessmen habitually offer a cup of coffee before starting to talk business. People drinking coffee in cafés often play games like backgammon or dominoes and smoke water pipes. These can be ordered from the waiter.

Some tea, please?	**shā**hy min **fadh**lek	شاي ، من فضلك؟
a lemon tea.	**shā**hy bilai**moon**	شاي بالليمون.
China/Indian tea.	**shā**hy **seen**y/**hin**dy	شاي صيني/هندي.
A coffee with milk, please.	ge**ha**wa bil-ha**leeb** min **fadh**lek	قهوة بالحليب، من فضلك.

a coffee with cream.	gehawa bi gishta	قهوة بقشطة.
a (black) coffee.	gehawa	قهوة.
an iced coffee.	gehawa muthellija	قهوة مثلجة.
a Turkish coffee.	gehawa turkeeya	قهوة تركي.
I'd like	eby ·	أريد
an orange juice with soda water.	aseer burtugāl bimiyāh souda	عصير برتقال بمياه صوده.
a glass of cold milk.	glās haleeb bārid	كوب حليب بارد.
a drink with plenty of ice.	aseer muthellej jidden	عصير مثلج جدا
a milkshake.	milkshaik	ملكشيك.
Have you	indek	هل عندك
any lemonade?	leemoonād	ليمونادة؟
a straw?	massāsa	مصاصة
Please bring me some dominoes.	eby doumeenou min fadhlek	أريد دومينو من فضلك.
I'd like a water pipe, please,	eby sheesha min fadhlek	أريد شيشة من فضلك.
with light tobacco/ strong tobacco.	bititin khefeef/bititin gowy	بتمباك خفيف/قوي.

VOCABULARY

beer	beera	بيره
canned beer	beera mu'alleba	بيرة معلبة
chocolate	shouklāta	شكولاتة
cordial	murattibāt	مرطبات
cup	finjān	فنجان
fruit juice	aseer	عصير فواكه
mineral water	miyāh ma'deneeya	مياه معدنية
syphon	saifoon	سيفون
tonic	tonik	مياه غازية
tumbler	kās	كأس.

Shopping

Buying Food

Eating out is fun but so is buying food in the various types of food shops and markets. If you are travelling through Arab countries independently or on an extended business trip these phrases will help you when shopping for food.

At the Butcher's

What kind of meat is that?	hādha el-lahem wish-hu [shin-hu]	ما هذا اللحم؟
What do you call that cut?	hādha el-gatu' shisma	ما هذا القطع؟
I'd like some steaks please	eby biftaik min fadhlek	أريد بفتيك من فضلك.
How much does that weigh?	kem el-wezin	كم الوزن؟
Will you please trim off the fat?	ikhidh el-shahem minha min fadhlek	قص الشحم من فضلك؟
Will you take the meat off the bone?	mumkin tijrim el-lahem min fadhlek	ممكن تجرم اللحم من فضلك؟
Will you mince it?	ifrimha min fadhlek	أفرمه من فضلك؟
Please slice it very fine/thick.	gatti'ha sherāyih khafeefa/meteena	قطعها شرايح رقيقة/سميكة.
I'll have a little more.	zeyyid-ha shwai	زيد شوية.
That's too much.	hādha zāyid	هذا كثير جدا.
Put it in a plastic bag.	hutt-ha bikees blāsteek min fadhlek	ضعها في كيس بلاستيك من فضلك.
Cut it, please.	gatti'ha min fadhlek	قطعها من فضلك.

Vocabulary

bacon	**bai**ken	بيكون
beef	lahem **aj**el	لحم عجل.
steak	bif**taik**	بفتيك
roast beef	roust**beef**	روستبيف
fillet of beef	fee**lait**	بيف فيلتو
brains	mukh	مخ
butcher	jez**zār**	جزار
cooking fat	semin	سمن
cutlets	ket**lait**	كستليتة
escalopes	eska**loub**	اسكالوب
lamb, leg of	**fukh**idh **dhā**ny	فخذ ضاني
lamb, shoulder of	**kit**ef **dhā**ny	كتف ضاني
liver	keb**da [cheb**da]	كبدة
kidneys	kil**wa [chil**wa]	كلاوي
sausages	**sous**ij	سوسج
tongue	li**sān**	لسان

At the Fishmonger's

Will you clean the fish?	**mum**kin tina**dh**if el-**si**mek [**si**mech]	ممكن تنظف السمك؟
Leave/take off the head/tail/fins, please.	khall/guss el-**rās**/el-**dhail**/ el-ze'**ā**nif, min **fadh**lek	اترك/قص الراس/الذيل/ الزعانف، من فضلك.
What kind of fish is that?	**shin**hu **hā**dha el-**si**mek	ما نوع هذا السمك؟

The names of fish vary according to region, many fish having local names.

Vocabulary

anchovies	en**shoo**ja	أنشوجة
bream	ebrā**mees**	ابراميس
carp	sheb**boot**	شبوط

clam	luzaig	لزيق
cod	gudd	قـد
crab	kāboorya	كابوريا
crayfish	salte'oon	سلطعون
eel	thi'bān el-māy	ثعبان الماء
fishmonger	semmāk	(سماك) بائع السمك
herring	simek el-zenja	سمك الزنجة
lobster	kerkend	كركند
octopus	ukhtuboot	اخطبوط
oysters	mahār	محار
perch	farukh	فرخ
pike	zenjoor	زنجور
plaice	simek moosa	سمك موسى
prawns	jembery	جمبري
salmon	selmoon	السلمون
sardines	serdeen	سردين
sole	simek moosa	سمك موسى
squid	sabbār	صبار
trout	simek el-etroot	سمك الأطروط
tuna	toona	تونة
turbot	simek el-turs	سمك الترسى
whitebait	sughār el-zenja	صغار الزنجة

At the Delicatessen/Grocer

What kinds of sausage have you got?	ai enwā' el-sousij elly indekum	أي أنواع السوسج عندكم؟
I'd like	eby	أريد
a peppery one.	sousij mufelfel	سوسج مفلفل.
one without garlic.	sousij bighair thoum	سوسج بغير ثوم.
one not too highly seasoned.	sousij galeel el-bahār	سوسج بشوية بهار.
I prefer	efadhdhil	أفضل
a coarse/smooth pâté.	bātai kheshina/batai nā'ima	باتية خشينه/ باتيه ناعمه

What kind of cheese is that?	hādhy el-jibna shismeha	ما نوع هذا الجبنة؟
Have you any goat's cheese?	indekum jibnet mā'iz	هل عندكم جبنة ماعز؟
Do you sell small pieces of cheese?	tebee' el-jibna bil-mufarrag	هل تبيع الجبنة بالمفرق؟
Are they ripe? May I taste?	hādhy nādhija. mumkin adhoog-ha	هل هي ناضجة؟ ممكن أذوق؟
Have you any biscuits?	indekum beskout	عندكم بسكوت؟
Do you sell cornflakes?	tebee' kourn felaiks	هل تبيع كورن فليكس؟
I'll take a little of each salad.	atny shweyya min kill nou' salāta	أعطني شيئاً من كل نوع صلاطة.
Do you have any tomato purée?	indekum tumātim mu'alliba	عندكم طماطم معلبة؟
Have you a jar of olives?	indekum jarret zaitoon	عندكم جرة زيتون؟

VOCABULARY

bacon	lahem khenzeer	لحم خنزير
biscuits	beskout	بسكوت
bread	khubz	خبز
brush	fersha	فرشاة
butter	zibda	زبدة
cheese	jibna	جبنة
chocolate	shoukolata	شكولاتة
cleaning fluid	munadhdhif	منظف
coffee	gahwa [gehawa]	قهوة
crisps	batāta magleeya [chibs]	بطاطه مقلية
detergent	munadhdhif	منظف
disinfectant	mutahher [mu'aggim]	مطهر
dried fruit	maiwa mejeffifa	فواكه مجففة
duster	manfidha	منفضة

eggs	baidh [dahāry]	بيض
flour	tuheen	طحين
garlic sausage	sijeg biththoum	سجق بالثوم
grocer	baggāl	بقال
ham	jāmboun	جامبون
herbs	a'shāb	أعشاب
jam	mrabba	مربى
macaroni	magrouna	مقرونة
margarine	marjereen	مرجرين
matches	kibreet [shakhāta]	كبريت
milk	haleeb	حليب
mustard	mistarda	مستردة
oil	zait	زيت
olives	zaitoon	زيتون
paper napkins	mehārim wareg [kleeneks]	محارم ورق
pepper	filfil	فلفل
pickles	mukhallelāt [turshy]	مخللات
rice	ruzz [timmen]	رز
salt	mileh	ملح
smoked fish	simek mudekhkhen	سمك مدخن
spaghetti	spegety	سبكتي
sugar	sukker [shiker]	سكر
tea	shāhy [chāy]	شاي
tinned food	ekil mu'alleb	اكل معلب
vinegar	khall	خل
washing powder	mes-hoog el-gheseel [pouder]	مسحوق الغسيل

CHEESES

Although there is not a great variety of cheese in Arab countries it is a staple ingredient of most meals, including breakfast. The main cheeses are:

| جبنة ماعز. | jibnet mā'iz | white goat's milk cheese |

مش.	mish	curd cheese
جبنة اريش.	jibnet areesh	salty, rich cheese
جبنة حلوم.	jibnet heloom	cottage cheese

At the Greengrocer and Fruiterer's

Is the melon ripe?	el-buteekh nādhij	هل البطيخ ناضج؟
How many will make a kilo?	el-kailo kem wihda	الكيلو كم وحدة؟
It's for eating today/tomorrow.	neby nākilha el youm/bukra	هذا للاكل اليوم / غدا.
Will you please weigh this?	ouzinha min fadhlek	من فضلك أوزن هذا؟
This lettuce is not very fresh.	el-khess hādha moob tāzij	هذا الخسة ليست طازجة.
Are these apples crisp?	el-tiffāh mugarresh	هل هذا التفاح مقرمش؟
Have you got a stronger bag?	indekum kees agwa min hādha	هل عندك كيس أقوى من هذا؟
I will put it in my carrier.	ahutta fy shantety	أحطه في شنطتي.
Have you got a box?	indekum kertoun	هل عندك كرتونة؟

Vocabulary

apples	tiffāh	تفاح
apricots	mishmish	مشمش
artichoke	khershouf	خرشوف
asparagus	el-helyoon	الهليون
aubergines	bādhinjān	باذنجان
avocados	abookādo	أبوكادو
banana	mouz	موز
beans, broad	fool	فول

beans, French	**fasoulya**	فاصوليا خضراء
beans, runner	**loobya**	لوبيا حمراء
beetroot	**shelgham**	بنجر
blackberry	**toot**	توت عليق
cabbage	**kern**eb	كرنب
carrots	**jizer**	جزر
cauliflower	gan**beet**	قنبيط
cherry	**kerez**	كرز
chestnut	**kesh**tena	الكستناء
cress	jer**jeer**	جرجير
cucumber	khiy**ār**	خيار
date	**tamur**	تمر
fig	**teen**	تين
garlic	**thoum**	ثوم
grapefruit	graib**froot**	جريب فروت
grapes	**ineb**	عنب
greengages	ber**goog akh**dher	برقوق أخضر
hazelnuts	**bin**dug	بندق
leeks	ker**rāth**	كراث
lemons	**laimoon**	ليمون
lettuce	**khess**	خسة
melon	**raggy** [**rejjy**] [**shemām**]	شمام
onions	**busel**	بصل
oranges	burte**ghāl**	برتقال
peaches	**khoukh**	خوخ
pears	**kem**thery [arne'**out**]	كمثرى
peas	**bājilla**	بازلاء
pineapple	**enanās**	أناناس
plums	**bergoug**	برقوق
potatoes	**betāta**	بطاطة
radishes	**fijil**	فجل
raspberry	**toot**	توت
rhubarb	**reebās**	ريباص
spinach	**spināj**	سبانخ
strawberries	**ferāwla**	فراولة
sweet corn	**dhi**ra **safra**	درة صفراء
sweet pepper	**filfil hilu**	فلفل حلو
tangerines	**yoosefen**dy	يسفندي

| tomatoes | tumātim | طماطم |
| turnips | lift | لفت |

Other Shops

In Arab countries shops usually close during the middle of the day for two to three hours and stay open till late. These hours often vary according to the season. In the hot months of summer they may remain closed all afternoon. Most travellers will know that one of the most colourful shopping areas of any town is the souk. This is a market, usually in a maze of little streets where artisans and small shopkeepers offer the shopper everything from antiques to spices. The word *sook* (*soug* in the phonetic transcript) signifies 'shops', 'bazaar' or 'market'. A large shop or store built on European lines is called a *makhzen*.

I want to go shopping.	ebarooh lil-soog	أريد أن اذهب إلى السوق.
Where are	wain	أين
the best shops?	ahsen soog	أحسن سوق؟
the cheaper shops?	erkhas soog	أرخص سوق؟
Where is the market?	wain el-soog el-sha'by	أين السوق؟
When do you close?	mita teghlig [tisekkir]	متى تغلق؟
Is there a grocer's near here?	feeh dukkān greyyib ala hina	هل يوجد دكان قريب من هنا؟

VOCABULARY

antique shop	mehall enteekāt	محل انتيكات
art gallery	ma'radh fenoon	معرض فنون
baker	khabbāz	خباز
bank	benk [masraf]	بنك [مصرف]
beauty salon	saloun tejmeel	صلون تجميل
bookshop	mekteba	مكتبة
butcher	jezzār	جزار

chemist	saideleeya	صيدلية
confectionery	haleweeyāt	حلويات
dairy	mehall elbān	محل ألبان
delicatessen	mekhallelāt	مخللات
department store	makhzen kebeer	محل كبير
dry cleaner	tendheef ala el-bukhār	تنظيف على البخار
fishmonger	mehall simek [simech]	محل سمك
greengrocer	khudhrajy	خضرجي
grocer	baggāl	بقال
hairdresser	hellāg	مصفف الشعر
hardware store	mehall edewāt menzeleeya	محل ادوات منزلية
jeweller	sayigh [jewāhiry]	جواهرجي
newsagent	mehall jerāyid	محل جرائد
optician	mehall nedhārāt	محل نظارات
photographer	musowwir	مصور
shoemaker	jezmejy	جزمجي
shoe shop	mehall ahdhiya	محل أحذية
stationer	mekteba	مكتبة
tailor	kheyyāt	خياط
tobacconist	mehall sejāyir	محل سجاير
toy shop	dukkān el-el'āb	دكان الالعاب
travel agency	mekteb el-siyāha	مكتب السياحة
watchmaker	mehall sā'āt	محل ساعات
wine merchant	mehall nebeedh	محل نبيذ

Buying Clothes

I'm just looking, thank you.	eshoof bess, shukren	انني اتفرج فقط ، شكرا.
Please show me some shirts.	min fadhlek rāweeny ba'dh el-gumsān	من فضلك أريني بعض القمصان.
plain/coloured/striped.	sāda/mulowwen/mukhattat	سادة/ملون/ مخطط.
with long/short sleeves.	bikum toweel/bikum guseyyir/	بكم طويل/ بكم قصير/
in cotton.	gutun	قطن.

My size is . . .	mugāsy . . .	...قياس
My collar size is . . .	mugās yākhety . . .	...مقاس ياقتي
This colour does not suit me.	mā yināsibny hādha el-loun	...هذا اللون لايناسبني
It is not my style.	el-modail mā yināsibny	.المديل لايناسبني
I want something more casual.	eby shai khefeef	.أريد شيء خفيف
Can I return it if it is unsuitable?	mumkin erajji'ha idha ma kān munāsib	ممكن أرجعها إذا ما عجبت؟
May I have a receipt?	mumkin te'ateeny el-wasel	ممكن تعطيني الوصل؟
It does not fit.	mā yirhem [mahoob mugāsy]	.لا تناسب
It is too large/small/ narrow/wide.	hādha killish kebeer/sugheer/ dheyyig/areedh	هذا كبير جدا/صغير جدا/ ضيق جدا/ واسع جدا.
Can you show me something else?	mumkin eshoof shai thāny	ممكن أري شيئا آخر؟
The zip is stuck/ broken.	el-sehhab atlāna/ meksoora	.السوستة عطلانة/مكسورة

VOCABULARY

MATERIALS

camel hair	webur	وير الجمل
chiffon	sheefoun	شيفون
cotton	gutun	قطن
crepe	kraib	كريب
denim	jeenz	جينز
felt	jookh	جوخ
flannel	fanilla	فانلة
gaberdine	jeberdeen	جبردين

lace	dantail	دانتيل
leather	jild	جلد
linen	kettān	كتان
materials	gumāsh	قماش
nylon	nailoun	نيلون
poplin	boubleen	بوبلين
rayon	hareer sunā'y	حرير صناعي
satin	sātān	ساتان
silk	hareer	حرير
suede	shamwā	شاموا
taffeta	tafeta	تفتاة
tweed	tweed	تويد
velour	gumāsh	قماش حريري
velvet	gudheefa	قطيفة
wool	soof	صوف
worsted	gumash soofy	قماش صوفي

MEASUREMENTS

arm	dhirā' [yed]	ذراع
chest	sadur	صدر
hip	radf	ردف
leg	sāg	ساق
length	tool	طول
neck	raguba	رقبة
waist	khasur	خصر

COLOURS

beige	baij	بيج
black	eswed	أسود
blue	ezrag	أزرق
brown	bunny	بني
green	akhdhar	أخضر
mauve	mouf	موف
orange	burteghāly	برتقالي

pastel colours	elwān bāstel	ألوان بلستل
pink	wardy	وردي
red	ahmer	أحمر
strong colours	elwān guweeya	ألوان فاقعة
violet	benefsejy	بنفسجي
white	ebyadh	أبيض
yellow	asfar	أصفر

ITEMS OF CLOTHING

anorak	mi'taf jildy	معطف جلدي
bathing hat	bounai lil-baher	بونية للبحر
bathrobe	burnus	برنس
belt	hizām	حزام
blazer	jākaita blaizer	جاكته بليزر
blouse	belowza	بلوزة
boots	boot	بوت
bra	sityān [sedreeya]	ستيان
briefs	kailout	كيلوت
buckle	ibreema	إبزيمة
button	zerār [zirr]	زرار
caftan	gaftān	قفطان
cap	kāskita	كاسكتة
cardigan	sitret soof	سترة صوف
coat	mi'taf [bālto]	معطف
dinner jacket	bedlet smouking	بدلة سموكنج
dress	fustān	فستان
elastic	mughāt	مغاط
girdle	hizām	حزام
gloves	kefoof	كفوف
gym shoes	hidhā riyādheeya	حذاء رياضي
handkerchief	mendeel	منديل
hat	gub'a	قبعة
jacket	jākaita	جاكتة
jeans	benteloun jeenz	بنطلون جينز
jumper	beloufer	بلوفر
negligé	roub	روب

nightdress	gumees noum [nefnoof]	قميص نوم
overcoat	mi'taf	معطف
panties	kailout	كيلوت
pants suit	kelsoun	كلسون
pocket	jaib	جيب
press stud	kebsool melābis	كبسول ملابس
pullover	beloufer	بلوفر
pyjamas	beejāma	بيجامة
raincoat	mi'taf mutar	معطف مطر
sandals	na'āl	صندل
scarf	esharb [charghed]	اشارب
shirt	gumees	قميص
shoelaces	rubāt ahdhiya	رباط أحذية
shoes	hidha [gunādir]	حذاء
shorts	shourt	شورت
skirt	joob	جوب
slip	shilha	شلحة
slippers	shebsheb	شبشب
stockings	joorāb	شراب حريمي
suit (man's)	bedla	بدلة
suit (woman's)	fustān	فستان
suspenders	hammāla	حمالة
swimsuit	māyo	مايوه
thread	khait	خيط
tie	krafāt [rubta]	كرافات
tights	joorāb hereemy tuweel	شراب حريمي طويل
trousers	bentaloun	بنطلون
T-shirt	gumees khefeef	قميص خفيف
twinset	blowza wa sitra	بلوزة وسترة
underpants	libās	لباس
vest	fānilla	فانلة
waistcoat	sudairy	صديري
zip	sehhāb	سحاب

At the Shoe Shop

I want a pair of	eby	أريد
shoes.	gunādir	حذاء خفيف
evening shoes.	hidha el-sahera	حذاء السهرة.
moccasins.	jildy	حذاء جلدي.
boots.	boot	بوت.
suede shoes.	shemwa	حذاء خيش.
slippers.	shebsheb	شبشب.
sandals.	na‘āl	صندل.
canvas shoes.	khaish	حذاء خيش

My size is . . .	mugāsy	قياسي ...

I need	eby	أريد
a broad/narrow fitting.	mugās wāsi‘/dheyyig	مقاس واسع/ضيق.

I want	eby hidhā	أريد حذاء
high heels.	bika‘b āly	بكعب عالي
low heels.	bika‘b wāty	بكعب واطي
flat-heeled shoes.	bika‘b musattah	بكعب مسطح
leather-soled shoes.	bika‘b jild	بكعب جلد
rubber-soled shoes.	bika‘b kāwchook	بكعب كاوتشوك
cork-soled shoes.	bika‘b fileen	بكعب فلين

These are not comfortable.	hādhy ghair mureeha	إنها غير مريحة.

May I try the other shoe?	mumkin ejarrib el-thāny	ممكن أقيس الحذاء الآخر؟

Have you got a shoehorn?	indek garen	هل عندك قرن؟

They are not my style.	hādhy ghair munāsiba	إنها غير مناسبة.

Have you any other colours?	indek elwān thānya	هل عندك ألوان أخرى؟

How much are they?	bikem hādhouly	بكم هي؟

This is expensive.	hādhy ghālya	هذا غال.
I'll wear them now. Will you please wrap up my old shoes?	elbis-ha helheen. liff el-gedeema min **fadhlek**	البسها الآن. لف حذائي القديمة من فضلك؟
Do you sell shoe polish/shoe cleaner/shoe brushes?	tebee' asbāgh ahdhiya/ munadhdhif el-ahdhiya/fershet el-ahdhiya	هل تبيع أصباغ الأحذية/ منظف الأحذية/ فرشاة الأحذية؟

Tobacconist's

Have you any English cigarettes?	indek sejāyir inglaizeeya	هل عندك سجاير انجليزي؟
What tobacco is the most popular here?	el-nou' el-mer**ghoob** **shin**-hu	ما هو التبغ الشعبي هنا؟
Is the tobacco Virginian/French/ Egyptian/Turkish/ American?	el-dukhān fer**jeeny**/fe**rensy**/ **masry**/**turky**/ emreeky	هل الدخان فرجيني/فرنسي/مصري/ تركي/ أمريكي؟
Have you any filter tips/king size/menthol cooled?	indekum bfilter/**ha**jem kebeer/sejāyir na'**nā**'	هل عندك/ فم فلتر/ حجم كبير/ سجاير نعناع؟
Do you sell pipe tobacco?	tebee' **ti**tin [tebāko]	هل تبيع تباكو؟
May I see your selection of pipes?	**mum**kin e**shoof** ba'adh enwā' elbāybāt	ممكن أرى بعض أنواع البيابات؟
I'd like a cigar.	eby seejār	أريد سيجار.
Do you sell pipe cleaners?	tebee' mu**nadh**dhif bāyb	هل تبيع منظف بايب؟

A packet/carton of cigarettes, please.	ilba/khertoushet sijāyir min **fadh**lek	علبة/خرطوشة... سجاير ، من فضلك.
A box of matches, please.	**il**bet kib**reet** min **fadh**lek	علبة كبريت، من فضلك.

VOCABULARY

box	**il**ba	علبة
carton	kher**tou**sha	خرطوشة
case	sen**doog** [**il**ba]	صندوق
cigarette lighter	wellā'a [jed**dā**ha]	ولاعة
cleaner	mu**nadh**hdhif	منظف
flint	**ha**jer wellā'a	حجر ولاعة
gas	ghāz	غاز
lighter fluid	ghāz wellā'a	غاز ولاعة
matches	kib**reet**	كبريت
packet	**il**ba	علبة
pipe	baib	بايب
pouch	kees [chees]	باكو دخان بياب

Hardware Store and Electrical Goods

I'd like a saucepan/frying pan.	eby **hel**la/**mag**la	أريد حلة/مقلة
Have you a grill/charcoal?	**in**dek shew**wā**ya/**fa**hem	هل عندك شواية/فحم؟
I need a metal or plastic can for water.	eby **te**neka lil-māy min blās**teek** ou su**feeh**	أريد وعاء من البلاستيك او الصفيح للماء.
I should like a bucket, please.	eby **jer**del [**sa**tul] min **fadh**lek	أريد جردل. من فضلك.
Give me a ball of strong twine, please.	**at**ny **shil**la dou**bā**ra she**dee**da min **fadh**lek	أعطني شلة دويارة شديدة، من فضلك.

I need a tow rope and a hook.	eby **ha**bil wa khat**tāf** lil-**sa**heb	أريد حبل وخطاف للسحب.
I need a battery for my torch/radio.	eby ba**tā**rya lil-**kah**ruba/lil-**rā**dyo.	أريد بطارية للكهربة/للراديو.
Can you repair this?	**mum**kin ṭu**sa**lih **hā**dha	ممكن تصلح هذا؟

VOCABULARY

adaptor	wu**see**la	وصيلة
basket	**si**lla [zem**beel**]	سلة
battery	ba**tā**rya	البطارية
brush	**fir**sha	فرشاة
bulb	**lem**ba	لمبة
car radio	**rā**dyo sey**yā**ra	راديو السيارة
chamois leather	jild **shām**wa	جلد شموا
distilled water	**māy** mu**gat**tir	ماء مقطر
duster	nef**fā**dha	نفاضة
fork	**shou**ka [chin**gāl**]	شوكة
hammer	shā**koosh**	شاكوش
insulating tape	shu**reet** **ā**zil	شريط عازل
iron	**mik**wa	مكواة
kettle	gha**lā**ya [**kait**li]	غلاية
knife	sik**keen** [**si**cheen]	سكين
mallet	**mut**riga	مطرقة
penknife	**mut**wa [**si**cheen]	مطواة
percolator	mu**saf**fa	مصفاة
saw	min**shār**	منشار
scissors	mi**gass**	مقص
screwdriver	mi**fekk**	مفك
spoon	mil**'a**ga .	ملعقة
string	**ha**bil [khait]	حبل
tweezers	mil**gāt**	ملقاط
wire	silk	سلك
wrench	mif**tāh** **ra**but	مفتاح ربط

Chemist's

Do I need a doctor's prescription?	ehtāj **wus**fa tub**bee**ya	هل أحتاج تذكرة طبية؟
Is there an all-night chemist open?	feeh saide**lee**ya mu**nā**wiba	هل توجد صيدلية مناوبة؟
Can you make up this prescription?	**mum**kin tuha**dhir**-ly **hā**dhy el-**wus**fa el-tub**bee**ya	ممكن تحضر هذه الوصفة الطبية؟
When will it be ready?	**mi**ta tuha**dhir**-ha	متى تحضرها؟
Will you write down the instructions in English if possible?	**mum**kin tek**tib**-ly el-ta'lee**māt** bil-in**glai**zy	ممكن تكتب لي التعليمات بالانجليزي؟
Is this dangerous for children?	feeh kha**tar** lil-et**fāl**	هل هذا خطير للأطفال؟
Have you anything for a cold? a sore throat? a cough?	**in**dekum shai lil-zuk**kām** li-**elem** fil-**halg** lil-**kah**ha	هل عندك شيء للزكام؟ ألم في الحلق؟ السعلة؟
I'd like to buy a thermometer.	e**besh**tiry termou**mi**ter	اريد شراء تيرمومتر.
Would you please have a look at this cut/bruise?	min **fadh**lek **shuf** ha**dha** el-**ja**reh/el-**ked**ma	من فضلك شوف لي هذا الجرح/الكدمة.
What kind of bandage would be best?	**shin**-hu **ah**sen ru**bāt**	ما أحسن رباط؟
I've got an upset stomach. diarrhoea. indigestion a headache. sunburn.	**in**dy **elem** fy el-**mi**'da is-**hāl** **a**ser **had**hum su**dā**' **ha**reg min el-**shems**	عندي ألم في المعدة. إسهال. عسر هضم. صداع. حرق من الشمس.
I am constipated.	**in**dy im**sāk**	عندي إمساك.

Vocabulary

Medicines

antibiotic	mudhād hayewy	مضاد حيوي
aspirin	espeereen	أسبيرين
bandage	rubāt	رباط
band-aids	shereet lāsig	شريط لاصق
contraceptive	máni' lil-hamel	مانع للحمل
corn plaster	shereet lil-kālo	شريط للكالو
cough lozenges	louzinj lil-kahha	لوزينج للسعال
cough mixture	duwa lil-kahha	دواء للسعال
cotton wool	gutun tubby	قطن طبي
disinfectant	mutahhir	مطهر
ear drops	gatret ādhān	نقط للأذن
gargle	gharghara	غرغرة
gauze	shāsh	شاش
insect repellant	tārid lil-hasherāt	طارد للحشرات
iodine	youd	يود
iron pills	egrās mugawwy	أقراص مقوي
laxative	muleyyin	ملين
lip salve	dehān lil-jurooh	دهان للجروح
sanitary towels	fout wareg tubby	فوط ورق طبي
sedative	musekkin	مسكن
sleeping pills	huboob munowwima	حبوب منومة
thermometer	termoumiter	ترمومتر
tranquillizers	egrās muhdi-a	أقراص مهدئة
vitamins	feetāmeenāt	فيتامينات

Toilet Articles

after-shave	ba'ad el-hilāga	بعد الحلاقة
bath oil	zait lil-hammām	زيت للحمام
bath salts	emlāh lil-hammām	أملاح للحمام
cologne	kolounya	كلونيا

cream, cleansing	kreem ten**dheef**	كريم ، تنظيف
foundation	kreem e**sāsy**	كريم أساسي
moisturizing	mu**rattib**	مرطب
deodorant	mu**zeel** li**rāyihet** el-'areg	مزيل لرائحة العرق
emery board	me**bred** e**dhāfir** kir**ton**	مبرد أظافر كرتون
eye pencil	ga**lem** ku**hel** lil-'ain	قلم كحل للعين
eye shadow	dhill lil-'u**yoon**	ظل للعيون
face powder	**boud**ra lil-**wejeh**	بودرة للوجه
lipstick	rouj lil-she**fāyif**	روج للشفايف
mascara	ku**hel**	كحل
nailbrush	fer**sha** lil-e**dhāfir**	فرشاة للأظافر
nail file	me**bred** e**dhāfir**	مبرد أظافر
nail polish	mu**lemmi'** lil-e**dhāfir**	ملمع للأظافر
nail polish remover	mu**zeel** li-loun el-e**dhāfir**	مزيل للون الأظافر
nappies	ku**foola** lil-**tufil**	كفولة للطفل
nappy pins	de**bābees** lil-ku**foola**	دبابيس للكفولة
perfume	a**tur**	عطر
plastic pants	kee**lout** blā**steek**	كيلوت بلاستيك
razor	moos	موس
rouge	**ahmar** she**fa**	أحمر شفاة
safety pins	de**bābees** e**mān**	دبابيس أمان
scissors	mi**gass**	مقص
shampoo	**shām**bu	شامبو
shaving brush	fer**sha** lil-hi**lāga**	فرشاة للحلاقة
shaving cream	kreem lil-he**lāga**	كريم للحلاقة
soap	**sā**boun	صابون
sponge	**sfin**ja	سفنجة
suntan oil	zait lil-shems	زيت للشمس
tissues	ghi**yārāt** [kleeneks]	غيارات
toilet paper	**wareg** tu**wā**lait	ورق تواليت
toothbrush	fer**sha** lil-es**nān**	فرشاة للأسنان
toothpaste	ma'**joon** lil-es**nān**	معجون للأسنان
tweezers	mil**gāt** su**gheer**	ملقاط صغير

At the Photographer's

I'd like to buy a camera.	ebeshtiry **kā**mera	أريد شراء كاميرا.
A camera that is cheap and easy to use.	**kā**mera rukhee**sa** wa **seh**la lil-isti'**māl**	كاميرا رخيصة وسهلة الاستعمال.
Will you please check my camera?	min **fadh**lek 'ad**dil**-ly hal-**kā**mera	من فضلك أعدلي كاميرتي؟
The film is stuck.	el-**film** mez**noog**	الفيلم مزنوق.
The exposure meter is not working.	mig**yās** **fet**-hat el-'a**di**sa at**lān**	مقياس فتحة العدسة عطلان.
The flash does not work.	el-**flāsh** mā **yish**tughul	الفلاش لا يشتغل.
The film winder is jammed.	mif**tāh** leff el-film maha**shour**	مفتاح لف الفيلم محشور.
Can you do it soon?	**mum**kin tisalliha bisur'a	ممكن تصلحه بسرعة؟
Will you please process this film?	min **fadh**lek **ham**mudh **hā**dha el-**film**	من فضلك حمض هذا الفيلم.
I would like prints with a matt/glossy finish.	eby **su**war ghair **lā**mi'a/**lā**mi'a	أريد صور غير لامعة / لامعة.
I want some black and white/ colour/Polaroid film.	eby film **es**wed u e**byadh**/ mu**low**wen/**bou**leroid	أريد فيلم أسود وأبيض / ألوان / بولرويد.
Is this film for use in daylight or artificial light?	**yum**kin istikh**dām** el-film **hā**dha fy el-**dhou** el-'**ā**dy ou istu**nā**'y	هل يمكن استخدام الفيلم في الضوء العادي أو الاصطناعي؟
I need a light meter.	eby mig**yās** el-dhou	أريد مقياس الضوء.
How much is an electronic flash?	kem yi**kel**lif flāsh elek**trou**ny	بكم يكلف فلاش إليكتروني؟

Vᴏᴄᴀʙᴜʟᴀʀʏ

120 film	eflām miya w'ishreen	افلام ١٢٠
127 film	eflām miya w seb'a w'ishreen	افلام ١٢٧
135 film	eflām miya w khamsa wthelātheen	افلام ١٣٥
620 film	eflām sit miya w 'ishreen	افلام ٦٢٠
24 exposures	arbe'a w'ishreen soora	٢٤ صورة
36 exposures	sitta wthelātheen soora	٣٦ صورة
camera case	ilbet kamera	علبة كاميرا
cinefilm	film	فيلم
8mm/16mm	themanyet milim/sitta'esh milim	٨ ملم/١٦ ملم
fast film	film seree'	فيلم سريع
slow film	film baty	فيلم بطىء
flash bulb	lembet flāsh	لمبة فلاش
lens	adisa	عدسة
lens cap	ghuta el-adisa	غطاء العدسة
long-focus lens	adisa be'eedet el-boora	عدسة بعيدة البؤرة
photograph	soora	صورة
photographer	musowwir	مصور
range finder	dhābit el-mesāfa	ضابط المسافة
red filter	filter ahmer	فيلتر احمر
reflex camera	ālet tesweer ākisa	عالة تصوير عاكسة
shutter	munadhim fethat el-adisa	منظم فتحة العدسة
ultra-violet filter	filter foug el-benefsejy	فيلتر فوق البنفسجي
wide-angle lens	adisa mutessi'et el-zāwiya	عدسة متسعة الزاوية
yellow filter	filter asfer	فيلتر أصفر

Bookshop/Stationer's

Where are the books on art/history/ politics/sport?	wain feeh kutub el-fenn/el-tāreekh/ elsiyāsa/el-riyādha	على أي رف توجد كتب الفن/التاريخ/ السياسة/ الرياضة؟

Where are the guide books?	**wain** el-kātouloujāt	أين الكاتولوجات؟
I want a pocket dictionary.	eby gāmoos el-**jaib**	اريد قاموس الجيب.
Have you any English paperbacks?	**indek kutub jaib** inglaizeeya [dhāt eghlifa khefeefa]	هل عندك كتب جيب إنجليزية ذات اغلفة خفيفة؟
Do you sell second-hand books?	tebee' kutub musta'mila	هل تبيع كتب مستعملة؟
I want a map of the area.	eby khareetet el-**mantiga**	اريد خريطة المنطقة.
The scale of this one is too small.	migyās hādhy el-khareeta sugheer jidden	مقياس هذه الخريطة صغير جدا.
Have you got refills for this ballpoint pen?	**indek** enboob hiber jāf li hādha el-galem	هل عندك أنبوب حبر جاف لهذا القلم؟
Can you please keep the English newspaper for me every morning?	mumkin tehajiz-ly el-jereeda el-inglaizeeya kull sabāh	ممكن تحجز لي الجريدة الانجليزية كل صباح؟

Vocabulary

address book	**defter** anāween	دفتر عناوين
box of crayons	ilbet eglām mulowwena	علبة أقلام ملونة
carbon paper	wareg karboun	ورق كربون
cellophane	wareg el-seloufān	ورق السلوفان
drawing paper	wareg rasim	ورق رسم
envelopes	dhuroof	ظروف
exercise book	**defter medresy**	دفتر مدرسي
fountain pen	galem hiber	قلم حبر
glue	samugh	صمغ
greaseproof paper	wareg tuleffbah el-eshya el-deheneeya	ورق تلف به الأشياء الدهنية
ink	hiber	حبر

label	butāga	بطاقة
magazines	mejellāt	مجلات
notebook	mufekkira	مفكرة
notepaper	wareg resāyil	ورق رسائل
paste	ma'ajoon	معجون
pen	galem hiber	قلم حبر
pencil	galem rasās	قلم رصاص
pencil sharpener	berrāya	براية
playing cards	wareg li'eb	ورق لعب
postcards	kuroot bereed	كروت بوستة
rubber	mimhā	ممحاة
ruler	mistara	مسطرة
silver foil	wareg mufadhidh	ورق مفضض
sketchpad	keras esketch	كراسي سكتش
tissue paper	wareg kleeneks	ورق كلينكس
typewriter ribbon	shereet li-āla kātiba	شريط لآلة كاتبة
typing paper	wareg li-āla kātiba	ورق لآلة كاتبة
writing pad	blouk wareg	بلوك ورق

Buying Souvenirs

Are all these things made locally?	kill hādhy el-eshya mesnoo'a mehalleeyen	هل كل هذه الأشياء مصنوعة محليا؟
This is a nice straw hat.	hādhy gab'a jemeela	هذه قبعة قش جميلة.
I like this bag.	hādhy el-shenta hilwa	هذا الشنطة حلوة.
Have you any costume jewellery?	indek broushāt	عندك بروشات؟
I'm looking for bracelets.	edouwwir esāwir	أفتش على أساور.
I'd like to try on that ring.	eby egees hādha el-khātim	أحب أن أقيس هذا الخاتم.
What is this bracelet made of?	hādhy el-eswāra wish mesnoo' minah	من أي شيء مصنوعة هذه الأسورة؟

I collect copperware. Have you any pots?	ejma' ewāny nuhāsiyya. indek jarrāt	أجمع أوان نحاسية. عندك أباريق؟
I'd like some local pottery.	eby fukhār mehally	أريد فخار محلي.
Can you pack this carefully?	min fadhlek liff hādha zain	من فضلك لف هذا كويس.
Do you despatch things abroad?	hel tirsil eshya lil-khārij	هل ترسل اشياء للخارج؟
I'm just looking around.	etefarrej fagat	أنا أتفرج فقط.
I will come back later.	eberja' ba'ad shwai	راجع بعد قليل.
Can I leave a deposit on it and return tomorrow?	mumkin etruk areboon wa erja' bāchir	ممكن أترك عربون وأرجع بكرة؟
Do you take foreign cheques?	hel tigbel shaikāt ejnebeeya	هل تقبل شيكات اجنبية؟

VOCABULARY

bazaar	soog mehally	بازار
beads	khezer	خرز
brooch	broush	بروش
chain	silsila	سلسلة
cigarette lighter	wellā'a [jeddāha]	ولاعة
clock	sā'et hāyit	ساعة حائط
costumes	melābis	رداء
cuff links	zerāyir gumsān	زراير قمصان
doll	dumya	دمية
earrings	haleg [terāchy]	حلق
jewel box	ilbet jewāhir	علبة جواهر
leatherwork	masnoo'āt jildeeya	مصنوعات جلدية
music box	ilbet mooseega	علبة موسيقى
necklace	aged [glāda]	عقد
pewterware	beyooter	(بيتر) سلسلة قصدير

rosary	**sib**ha	سبحة
silverware	fu**dhee**ya	فضية
souvenir	tidh**kār**	تذكار
watchstrap	sair **sā**ʿa	أستيك ساعة
wristwatch	**sā**ʿet yed	ساعة يد .

Entertainment

Out for the Evening

Nightclubs

Which is the best nightclub here?	**wain ah**sen **mel**ha **laily** hina	ما احسن ملهى ليلي هنا؟
Where is there	**wain** feeh	اين يوجد
a place with dancing and a cabaret?	mu**kān** feeh **mar**gas wa kabārai	مكان فيه مرقص وكباري؟
a disco?	**dees**ko	ديسكو (مرقص)؟
an open-air dance?	**mar**gas fy el-**how**a el-**ta**lig	مرقص في الهوا الطلق؟
a nightclub with hostesses/belly dancers?	**mel**ha **laily** bimu**dhey**yifāt/ rāgi**sāt** sher**gee**ya	ملهى ليلي بمضيفات/راقصات شرقيات؟
Is there an entrance fee?	feeh rasim du**khool**	هل هناك رسم دخول؟
Does it include drinks?	hel **yesh**mil el mesh**roob**	هل هذا يشمل المشروب؟
What is the cost of drinks?	**kem** yukel**lif** el-mesh**roob**	كم يكلف المشروب؟
At what time does the show start?	**mita** yib**da** el-**ardh**	متى يبدأ العرض؟
Are the drinks at the bar cheaper?	hel elmesh**roob** fy el-**bār** er**khas**	هل المشروب في البار أرخص؟
I do not want a photograph.	**mā** eby **soo**ra	لا أريد صورة.
Would you like to dance?	tehib**been** targi**seen**	تحبين أن ترقصي؟

Cinemas

What is on at the cinema?	**shin**-hy el-eflām el-mou**joo**da	ما هي الأفلام؟
Have you got a guide to what's on?	**in**dek ber**nā**mej el-**seh**ra	هل عندك برنامج السهرة؟
Two stalls/circle/ amphitheatre, please?	mag'**adain** e**mām**/fy el-**bāl**koun/fy el-**sā**la, min **fadh**lek	مقعدين أماميين/ في البلكون في الصالة، من فضلك.
Will we have to queue for long?	**nā**gef fy el-saff **mud**da tu**wee**la	هل نقف في الصف لمدة طويلة؟
I want a seat near the front/at the back/in the middle.	eby **mag**'ad e**mām**y/**khal**fy/ **was**tāny	أريد مقعد قريب للأمام/ وراء/وسط.
Do I tip the usherette?	a'ty bakh**sheesh** lil'um**māl**	هل أعطي بقشيش للعمال؟
I'd rather sit over there.	e**fadh**dhil elj**loos** hi**nāk**	أفضل الجلوس هناك.
I have dropped something.	**tāh**-ly shai	سقط لي شيء.
Do they sell ice-cream?	yebee'**oon** dun**dur**ma [ais **kreem**]	هل يبيعوا بوظة (ايس كريم)؟
At what times does the main film start?	**mi**ta **yib**da el-film el-es**ā**sy	متى يبدأ الفيلم الأساسي؟
Will you please move over to the right/left.	min **fadh**lek **shwey**ya ye**meen**/shi**māl**	من فضلك شوية يمين/شمال.

Vocabulary

actor	mu**meth**thil	ممثل
actress	mu**meth**thila	ممثلة
director	**mukh**rij	مخرج
dubbing	doob**lāj**	دوبلاج
film	film	فيلم
interval	istirāha	أستراحة
producer	**mun**tij	منتج
projector	brou**jek**ter	بروجكتر
screen	**shā**sha	الشاشة
seat	**mag**'ad	مقعد
sound	sout	صوت
star	**ne**jim	نجم

Casino

What games are played here?	**shin**-hy el-el'āb el**mou**jooda **hi**na	ما هي الألعاب الموجودة هنا؟
What is the minimum stake in this room?	ish egall ri**hān** fy **hā**dha el-mu**kān**	ما أقل رهان في هذا المكان؟
Can I buy some chips?	**mum**kin esh**tir**y feesh	ممكن أشتري فيش؟
I should like . . . worth.	**at**ny bi . . .	أعطني بــ...
Excuse me, those are my chips.	**ā**sif **hā**dhy el-**feesh** ly	اسفه ، هذه الفيش لي.
Where can I cash my chips?	wain esteb**dil** el-**feesh**	أين أستبدل الفيش؟
I'm bust/that's the end of the game for me!	ef**lest**/**hā**dhy ne**hā**yet el-la'eb	أفلست/هذه نهاية اللعب!
I'll take another card.	**ā**khidh **kārt thā**ny	اخذ كارت آخر.
No more.	y**keff**y	يكفي.
Pass me the dice, please.	**'at**ny el-nard min **fadh**lek	أعطني النرد، من فضلك.

Vocabulary

ace	āş	أس
banker	wareg	ورق
bet	murāhena	مراهنة
cards	wareg li'eb	ورق لعب
clubs	subāty	سباتي
croupier	mudeer maiz el-gumār	مدير مائدة القمار
diamonds	deenāry	ديناري
evens	aded zoujy	عدد زوجي
hearts	kooba	كوبا
jack	el-weled	الولد
joker	jouker	جوكر
king	shāyib	الشايب
poker	bouker	بوكر
queen	melika	الملكة
spades	bestoony	البستوني

Out for the Day

On the Beach

Does one have to pay to use this beach?	isti'mâl hādha el-shāty bil-floos	هل استعمال هذا الشاطى بالفلوس؟
Is it clean?	el-shāty nudheef	هل الشاطى نظيف؟
How much does it cost to hire	kem ujret	كم أجرة:
a cabin?	el-kebeena	الكبينة؟
a deckchair?	kursy blāj	كرسي بلاج؟
an air mattress?	mertebet howa	مرتبة هواء؟
a sun umbrella	shemseeya	شمسية؟
per day/per week.	bil-laila/bil-isboo'	بالليلة/الاسبوع
Can I leave valuables in the cabin?	mumkin etruk eshya geyyima fy el-kābeena	ممكن اترك اشياء قيمة في الكبينة؟

Is the ticket valid all day?	el-**tedh**kira **s**āliha li-**tool** el-ne**h**ār	هل التذاكر صالحة لطول النهار؟
Does the beach slope steeply?	el-**sh**āty she**deed** el-inhi**d**ār	هل الشاطى شديد الانحدار؟
Is it safe for swimming?	el-si**b**āha e**m**ān	هل السباحة أمان؟
Are there any currents?	feeh teyā**r**āt	هل توجد تيارات؟
Is it safe to dive off the rocks?	el-**gh**atus min el-su**kh**oor e**m**ān	هل الغطس من الصخور أمان؟
Where is the fresh-water shower?	**wain** doosh el-**ma** el-**b**ārda	اين دوش الماء البارد؟
Have you any tar remover?	**in**dek mu**zeel** lil-zift	هل عندك مزيل للزفت؟
Can I hire a swimsuit/trunks?	**mum**kin isti'**j**ār **m**āyo/li**b**ās bahry	هل يمكن استئجار مايوه/ لباس بحر؟
I've hurt my foot. Have you any elastoplast?	**jer**aht **ga**demy. **in**dek **bles**ter	جرحت قدمي. هل عندك بلستر؟
Is there a lost property office?	feeh **mek**teb mefgoo**d**āt	هل يوجد مكتب مفقودات؟
Is there a children's beach club?	feeh **n**ādy lil-et**f**āl ala el-**sh**āty	هل يوجد نادي للأطفال على الشاطى؟
At what time are the keep fit classes?	**mi**ta ougāt **hi**sas el-ri**y**ādha	ما أوقات حصص الرياضة؟
Is there water ski tuition available?	feeh mu**der**rib te**zel**lug ala el-**ma**	هل يوجد مدرب تزلق على الماء؟
Do I have to know how to swim?	**l**āzim a'**arif** es**bah**	لازم أعرف اسبح؟
Where is the nearest beach shop?	**wain** e**grab** duk**k**ān ala el-**sh**āty	اين أقرب دكان على الشاطى؟

Have you got a life jacket?	indek sadreeyet el-nejāt	هل عندك صدرية النجاة؟
Is this a good place for skin diving?	hādha el-mukān munāsib lil-ghatus	هل هذا المكان مناسب للغطس؟
Help! I'm in difficulty.	ilhagoony! [el-nejda!]	الحقوني! [النجدة!]

VOCABULARY

beach ball	kura	كرة
cactus	sabbār	صبار
goggles	nadhārāt wāgiya	نظارات واقية
harpoon gun	bindugeeya li-said el-heetān	بندقية لصيد الحيتان
high tide	medd	المد
lilo	fershet houwa	فرشة هواء
low tide	jezer	الجزر
net	shebeka [shebicha]	شبكة
pedalo	beddālo	بدالو
pines	senouber	الصنوبر
promenade	nezha	نزهة
raft	touwwāfa	طوافة
rocks	sukhoor	صخور
rowing boat	merkeb mijdhāf	مركب بمجداف
sand	ramul	رمل
sandals	sandel [nu'ool]	صندل
sea	baher	بحر
seaweed	a'shāb bahreeya	أعشاب بحرية
shells	sadef	صدف
shingle	hasa	حصى
sun oil	zait el-shems	زيت للشمس
surfing	rukoob el-emwāj	رياضة ركوب الأمواج
surf board	touwwāfa	طوافة
underwater	taht el-ma	تحت الماء
waterski instructor	muderrib el-tezellug	مدرب التزلق على الماء
yacht	yakhet [sefeena bishrā']	يخت

Sightseeing

Where can I get a good guide book?	**wain** ehassil ala de**leel** siyāhy zain	اين أحصل على دليل سياحي جيد؟
Is there an excursion round the city?	feeh joula siyāheeya fy el-medeena	هل توجد جولة سياحية في المدينة؟
Is it a conducted party?	feeh murshideen	هل هناك مرشدين؟
Am I allowed to go round alone?	**mum**kin nitejouwwel bikaifna	هل لنا حرية الحركة؟
Where do I find an official guide?	**wain** elga **mur**shid siyāhy **ras**my	اين أجد مرشد سياحي رسمي؟
Is lunch included in the excursion price?	el-ghada mahasoob fy tekāleef el-joula	هل الغداء محسوب في تكاليف الجولة؟
Are the entrance fees extra?	resm el-dukhool zāyid	هل رسم الدخول زائد؟
Should I give a tip to the guide/driver?	a‘ty bakhsheesh lil-**mur**shid/lil-**sā**yig	هل أعطى بقشيش للمرشد / للسائق؟
I'd like to stay here longer.	ebageem fetra atwel hina	اريد ان اقيم فترة أطول هنا.
I'll meet the party later.	eltehig bilmejmoo‘a ba‘dain	سألتقي المجموعة فيمابعد.
Where will you be?	**wain** eshoofkum	اين أراكم؟
Will you please write it down?	iktiba min fadhlek	من فضلك أكتبه؟

In Churches/Mosques

Do ladies have to cover their heads?	lāzim el-sittāt yighattūn roos-hum	لازم الستات يغطين رؤوسهن؟

Is it all right to enter like this?	**mum**kin edkhul **ki**dha	هل أستطيع الدخول هكذا؟
Should I remove my shoes?	**lā**zim **en**za' hid**hāy**	لازم أخلع حذائي؟
Are slippers provided?	feeh she**bā**shib [mi**dās**]	هل هناك شباشب؟
When was this church/mosque built?	**mi**ta binyet **hā**dhy el-ke**nee**sa/el-**jā**mi'	متى بنيت هذه الكنيسة/ هذا المسجد؟
Who founded it?	**min**-hu elly **es**ses-ha (*fem.*)/**es**sesa (*masc.*)	من أسسها/ أسسه ؟
Are the stained glass windows original?	hel rusoo**māt** el nu**wā**fidh as**lee**ya	هل رسومات النوافذ أصلية؟
Is one allowed to go up the bell tower?	**yum**kin el-tu**loo'** ila el-**burj**	هل يمكن الطلوع إلى البرج؟
Is there a book about the building?	feeh ki**tāb** an el-**meb**na	هل يوجد كتاب عن المبنى؟
May I leave a small contribution?	**mum**kin eteb**erra'**	هل أتبرع؟

Vocabulary

abbey	dair	الدير
aisles	me**marr** fy wast el-ke**nee**sa	ممر في وسط الكنيسة
altar	**hai**kel el-ke**nee**sa	هيكل الكنيسة
arch	gous	قوس
basilica	bāzee**leek**	البازيليك
candle	**shema'**	شمع
cathedral	kātaid**rā**ya	الكاتدرائية
chapel	**mā'**bed su**gheer**	معبد صغير
choir	k**wāyr**	كواير
column	a**mood**	عمود
convent	dair lil-ekhe**wāt**	الدير
crucifix	sa**leeb**	صليب

crypt	sirdāb	سرداب
font	houdh el ma'moodeeya	حوض المعمودية
fresco	resm ala jibs	رسم على الجبس
monastery	dair [ribāt]	الدير
nave	sahen el-keneesa	صحن الكنيسة
rood	saleeb kebeer	صليب كبير
sculpture	nahet [timthāl]	النحت [تمثال]
shrine	dhureeh	ضريح

Art Galleries and Museums

Have you a catalogue/an illustrated catalogue?	indek ketālouj/ketālouj musouwwer	هل عندك كتالوج/ كتالوج مصور؟
Are there any plaster casts?	indekum temātheel jibs	هل عندكم تماثيل جبس؟
Do you sell slides?	tebee' slaidz	هل تبيع سليدز؟
Am I allowed to take photographs?	el-tesweer mesmooh	هل التصوير مسموح؟
May I use my tripod?	mumkin esta'mil el-hāmil	ممكن استعمل الحامل؟
Is the gallery open on Sundays?	gā'et el-funoon meftooha youm el-ahed	هل قاعة الفنون مفتوحة يوم الأحد؟
Is it free?	el-dukhool mejjāny	هل الدخول مجاني؟
Where can I find the Dutch School?	wain el-medresa el-houlendeeya	أين المدرسة الهولندية؟
Do you make photocopies?	ta'mel nusekh	هل تعمل نسخ؟
Where is the library?	wain el-mekteba	أين المكتبة؟

Vocabulary

antique books	kutub gedeema	كتب قديمة
china	el-seen	الصين
costumes	melābis	لباس
drawing	resim	الرسم
engraving	nagish	النقش
etching	hafer el-kleesheehāt	حفر الكليشيهات
frame	itār	إطار
furniture	ethāth	الفرش
jewels	jewāhir	جواهر
lithograph	tabe' leethoughrāfeeya	طبع ليثوغرافية
miniature	soora musaghira	صورة مصغرة
porcelain	khezif seeny	خزف صيني
pottery	fukhār	فخار
silverware	fudhdha	فضة

Historical Sights

Is the place far?	el-mukān be'eed	هل المكان بعيد؟
Can I wait here till you return?	mumkin entadhir hina hetta terja'oon	ممكن انتظر هنا حتى ترجعوا؟
Is there a souvenir stall?	feeh kushk soofeneer	هل يوجد كشك سوفنير؟
Where can we get a cold drink?	wain ehassil ala murattibāt	اين احصل على مرطبات؟
Is there a plan of the grounds?	feeh khareeta lil-mantiga	هل توجد خريطة للمنطقة؟
I would like to walk round the gardens.	ebetemeshsha fy el-hedāyig	اريد ان اتمشى في الحدائق؟

VOCABULARY

amphitheatre	mu**der**rij	مدرج
aqueduct	**gun**tura	قنطرة
armour	**dire'**	درع
battlements	shere**fāt**	شرفات
cannon	**mid**fa'	مدفع
castle	**gasur**	القصر
catacombs	serā**deeb** el-em**wāt**	سراديب الأموات
column	a**mood**	عمود
courtyard	**sāha**	ساحة
crossbow	menje**neeg**	منجنيق
fort	**gal'a**	قلعة
forum	**sāha**	ساحة
fountain	nā**foora**	النافورة
gate	bou**wāba**	بوابة
mosque	**jāmi'** [**mesjid**]	جامع [مسجد]
old city	me**dee**na ge**dee**ma	المدينة القديمة
palace	**gasur**	قصر
pyramids	eh**rām**	الأهرام
ruins	ā**thār** [khe**rāyib**]	آثار [خرائب]
sphinx	ebu el-**houl**	أبو الهول
tomb	**mag**bera	مقبرة
viaduct	**jiser**	جسر
wall	**soor**	سور

Sport

The most important mass sport in Arab countries is football but, like other sports, it is a newly acquired interest. Consequently there are few big stadiums and no international teams. Tennis and basketball are also catching on and so are water sports, especially in the countries bordering the Mediterranean. Horse racing, too, has its followers. In most tourist centres the leisure activities popular in Europe are often, though not widely, available.

Football

Where is the stadium?	**wain** el-**mel**'ab [stādyoum]	اين الملعب؟
Could you show me the way to get there?	**mum**kin tedel**leeny** ala el-tu**reeg**	ممكن تدلني على الطريق؟
Should I book tickets?	**lā**zim e**ha**jiz ted**hā**kir	لازم احجز تذاكر؟
Will it be very crowded?	ye**seer** feeh izdi**hām**	هل يكون مزدحما؟
Who is playing?	**min**-hu elli **yil**'ab	من يلعب؟
Is there a local team?	feeh fe**reeg** me**hally**	هل هناك فريق محلي؟
I want a ticket for the main stand/a place under cover/in the open.	eby **ted**hkira fy el-e**mām**/**mag**'ad mug**hat**ta/mek**shoof**	اريد تذكرة في الأمام. مقعد مغطى/ مكشوف.
I should like a programme.	eby ber**nā**mej	اريد البرنامج.

VOCABULARY

attack	hu**joom**	هجوم
defence	di**fā'**	دفاع
goalkeeper	**hāris** el-**merma**	حارس المرمى
goalposts	**amood** el-**merma**	عمود المرمى
halfway line	el-**khatt** el-**nusfy**	الخط النصفي
penalty area	**men**tagat ha**rām**	منطقة حرام
players	el-**lā'ibeen**	اللاعبين
referee	**hakem**	حكم
team	fe**reeg**	فريق

Race Meetings

I want a ticket for the race meeting/a grandstand seat, please.	eby **tedh**kiret si**bāg** el-**khail/mag**'ad fy el-mu**der**rej, min **fadh**lek	أريد تذكرة سباق الخيل/ مقعد في المدرج، من فضلك.
Where can I place a bet?	**wain** mumkin e**rāhin**	أين يمكن أراهن؟
What are the odds on number 5?	ish el-ihti**mālāt** ala **ragum kham**sa	ما هي الاحتمالات على رقم ٥؟
Which is the favourite?	**shin**-hu el-hu**sān** el-mu**raj**jah **fouzah**	ما هو الحصان المرجح فوزه؟
I will back the outsider.	e**rāhin** ala el-hu**sān** el-**khāyib**	سأراهن على الحصان الخايب.
Is the jockey well known?	el-**jouky** ma'a**roof**	هل الجوكي معروف؟

VOCABULARY

camel	jimel [nāga, *pl.* ibil]	جمل [ناقة]
course	maidān	ميدان [حلبة]
filly	muhra	مهرة
flat	sibāg doon hewājiz	سباق دون حواجز
horse	husān	حصان
hurdles	hewājiz	حواجز
jockey	jouky	جوكي
owner	sāhib	صاحب
rails	hewājiz	حواجز
stable	istabl	إسطبل
starting gate	nugtet intilāg	نقطة الانطلاق
trainer	murowwidh	مروض

Tennis

Is there a tennis club near here?	feeh nādy el-tenis gereyyib	هل يوجد ناد التنس قريب؟
Where is the championship held?	wain tekoon mubārāt el-butoola	أين ستكون مباراة البطولة؟
How can I get some tickets?	wain ehassil 'ala tedhākir	كيف أحصل على تذاكر؟
Should I arrive early?	lāzim āsil mubekkir	هل لازم أوصل مبكرا؟
Who is playing?	min-hu elli yil'ab	من يلعب؟
I want to watch the men's singles/doubles/ mixed doubles.	ebeshāhid mubārāt ferdeeya/mubārāt zoujeeya/mubārāt zoujeeya mukhtalut	أريد أن أشاهد مباراة فردية / مباراة زوجية / مباراة زوجية مختلط.
How do you score in Arabic?	kaif tesejjil el-nugāt bil-'areby	كيف تسجل النقط بالعربي؟

Shall we toss for service?	khalna **neg**tari'	دعنا نقترع
Let's adjust the net.	khal ne'**ad**dil el-**she**beka	سنعدل الشبكة.
It's too high/too low.	hija 'aliya/mun**kha**fidha	إنها عالية جدا/ منخفضة جدا.
That was out/in/on the line.	el-**ku**ra **kha**rija/**da**khila/'ala el-khatt	الكرة خارجة/ داخلة/ على الخط.
Good shot.	mum**taz**	ممتاز.
Will you keep the score?	**mum**kin te**ha**riz el-**nu**gat	ممكن تحرز النقط؟
Change ends.	teb**deel**	تبديل.

VOCABULARY

backhand	**dhar**ba bi**dha**her el-**mid**hrab	ضربة بظهر المضرب
forehand	**dhar**bet el-**ku**ra min el-**ji**ha el-**yum**na	ضرب الكرة من الجهة اليمنى
racquet	**mid**hrab	مضرب
smash	**dhar**ba gu**wee**ya	ضربة قوية
tennis ball	**ku**ret **te**nis	كرة تنس
umpire	**ha**kem	حكم
volley	dharb el-**ku**ra **ga**bul la te**miss** el-arudh	ضرب الكرة قبل أن تمس الأرض.

Golf

Is there a golf course nearby?	feeh mel'ab goulf **grey**yib	هل يوجد ملعب جولف قريب؟
Does one have to be a member?	**la**zim e**koon** adhuw	لازم تكون عضو؟
Is there temporary membership?	feeh 'udh**wee**ya mu**wag**geta	هل توجد عضوية مؤقتة؟

How much does it cost to play?	bikem el-la'eb	بكم اللعب؟
I'd like a caddy.	eby hāmil edewāt el-goulf	أريد حامل أدوات الجولف.
Are there any trolleys for hire?	yumkin isti'jār trouly	هل يمكن استئجار ترولي؟
I'd like to speak to the professional.	ebekellim el-lā'ib el-muhterif	أريد أن أتكلم مع اللاعب المحترف.
Can you give me a lesson now?	mumkin ākhidh dersy el-heen	ممكن آخذ درس الآن؟
Will you play a round with me?	mumkin til'ab dour ma'y	ممكن تلعب دور معي؟
My approach shots are weak.	ramyety dha'eefa	رميتي ضعيفة.
I'll do some putting while I wait for you.	edhull etemarran lain tijy	سأتمرن إلى أن تأتي.
Can I hire some clubs?	yumkin isti'jār asa	هل يمكن إستئجار عصا؟
May I have a scorecard?	atny kārt li-tesjeel el-nugat min fadhlek	أعطني كرت لتسجيل النقط من فضلك.

VOCABULARY

bunker	shark	شرك
club house	bait el-nādy	بيت النادي
golf bag	hageebet goulf	حقيبة الجولف
green	bug'a yeghatteeha el-ishib	بقعة يغطيها العشب
hook	dharba	ضربة
irons	midhrab hadeed	مضرب
mashie	asa el-goulf	عصا للجولف
par	te'ādul [tekāfu']	تعادل [تكافؤ]
rough	arudh wa'ira	أرض وعرة
slice	dharb khata	ضرب خطأ

Water-skiing

I have never skied before.	**mā** teze**llejt** ala el-ma min **ga**bul	لم أتزلج على الماء من قبل.
I am not a good swimmer.	**mā**ny seb**bāh mā**hir	لست سباحا ماهرا.
Do I wear a life jacket?	**el**bes se**dār** el-ni**jāt**	هل ألبس صدار النجاة؟
Will you please help me to put on the skis?	min **fadh**lek sā**'id**ny fy libs el-zah**loo**ga	من فضلك ساعدني في لباس الزحلوقة.
Please pass me the rope.	**at**ny el-**ha**bil min **fadh**lek	أعطني الحبل من فضلك.
May I ride on the speed boat?	**mum**kin er**kab zou**rag el-si**bāg**	ممكن أركب زورق السباق؟
Can I borrow a wetsuit?	**mum**kin es**tlif bed**let el-**gha**tus	ممكن أستلف بدلة الغطس؟
I'm ready now.	ana **hā**dhir el-**heen**	أنا مستعد الآن.
Just a moment.	**lah**dha	لحظة.

VOCABULARY

aquaplane	louh el-ma	لوح الماء
bathing hat	bou**naih** el-**ba**her	بونيه البحر
goggles	nadh**ā**rāt el-**ba**her	نظارات البحر
(to) jump	ga**fuz**	قفز
monoski	teze**lluj** 'ala rijl **wāh**da	تزلج على رجل واحدة
slalom	si**bāg** skee	سباق سكي

Riding

Is there a riding stable here?	feeh istabl li rukoob el-khail hina	هل توجد إسطبل لركوب الخيل هنا؟
Can I hire a horse for riding?	mumkin este'jir khail lil-rukoob	ممكن استاجر خيل للركوب؟
Do you give lessons?	te'ty duroos	هل تعطي دروس؟
I'd like to go for a ride.	ebarkab khail	اريد ان اركب خيل.
I'd like a quiet horse.	eby husān hādy	اريد حصانا هادئا.
Have you any ponies?	indekum muhoor	هل عندكم مهور؟
Will an instructor accompany the ride?	feeh mudarrib yurāfigna	هل سيرافقنا مدرب؟
I'd like to practise jumping.	ebatedarreb ala el-gafuz	اريد التدريب على القفز.
I am an experienced rider/a novice.	ana rākib muhannek/mubtedy	انا راكب محنك/مبتدىء.
Do you have English saddles?	indekum esrāj inglaizeeya	هل عندكم أسراج إنجليزية؟
This horse has gone lame.	hādha el-husān arej	هذا الحصان أعرج.
The girth is too loose.	el-hizām ghair meshdood	الحزام غير مشدود.
Will you please adjust my stirrups/girth?	min fadhlek addil el-rikāb/el-hizām	من فضلك ضبط ركابي/حزامي.
Will you hold my horse while I get on?	mumkin temsik el-husān hatta arkeb	ممكن تمسك الحصان حتى اركب؟
Will you help me to get on?	mumkin tesā'idny fy el-rukoob	ممكن تساعدني في الركوب؟

Vocabulary

bit	shi**kee**met el-li**jām**	شكيمة اللجام
bridle	li**jām**	لجام
girth	hi**zām**	حزام
harness	**ta**gum	طقم
hoof	**hā**fir	حافر
mare	**fa**res	فرس
martingale	sair	سير
reins	sair el-li**jām**	سير اللجام
stallion	hu**sān** [**fa**hel]	حصان [فحل]
withers	**kā**thiba [**ghā**rib el-**fa**res]	كاثبة [غارب الفرس]

Fishing

Where can I get a permit to fish?	**wain** ehassil ala **rukh**sa li-said el-**si**mek	أين احصل على رخصة لصيد السمك؟
Is there big game fishing in this area?	el-**said zain** hina	هل الصيد جيد هنا؟
How much does a day's fishing cost?	kem ti**kel**lif el-said bil-**youm**	كم تكلف الصيد باليوم؟
Where can I get some bait?	**wain** elga **tu'**am li-said el-**si**mek	أين أجد طعم لصيد السمك؟
What is the best time of day to go out?	**mita** ahsen wagt lil-tu**loo'**	ما احسن وقت للخروج؟
Are there any boats that will take me deep sea fishing?	**feeh** zu**wā**rig mshān said el-**si**mek min a'**māg** el-**ba**her	هل توجد زوارق لصيد السمك من أعماق البحر؟
Do they provide tackle?	**feeh in**dehum ede**wāt** el-said	هل لديهم أدوات الصيد؟

| Is it safe to skin dive here? | **yum**kin el-**ghat**us hina | هل يمكن الغطس هنا؟ |
| Where can I hire diving equipment? | **wain** yumkin este'jir edewāt el-**ghat**us | أين يمكن استأجر ادوات غطس. |

VOCABULARY

fishing season	**fas**ul said el-**sim**ek	فصل صيد السمك
flippers	za'nifa	زعنفة
float	āyim	عائم
fly	dhibāba [**hal**lig]	ذبابة [حلق]
gaff	khuttāf	خطاف
goggles	nadherāt el-**bah**er	نظارات البحر
hook	sun**nār**a	صنارة
line	khait	خيط
lure	tu'am lil-tegh**reer** wa el-ghe**wāy**a	طعم للتغرير والغواية
net	shebeka [**sheb**icha]	شبكة
oxygen cylinder	si**lind**er el-okseejeen	سلندر الاكسيجين
reel	**bak**era [khait]	بكرة [خيط]
snorkel	**snour**kel	سنوركل
spinner	ghez**zāl**	غزال
weights	eth**gāl**	اثقال

Shooting

Where can I shoot?	**wain** yumkin es**tād**	أين يمكن أن اصطاد؟
Do I need a licence?	eh**tāj** li-**rukh**sa	هل احتاج لرخصة؟
I'd like to borrow a 12-bore shotgun.	ebeste'**eer** bunde**gee**ya iyār ethna'esh	أريد أن استعير بندقية (عيار)١٢.
I have my own rifle.	**ind**y bunde**gee**ya	عندي بندقيتي الخاصة
Is there a shooting party I could join?	**yum**kin el**teh**ig bi-je**mā**'a fy el-**said**	هل يمكن أن التحق بجماعة في الصيد؟

| Is there a clay pigeon shoot? | **in**dekum el-re**mā**ya ala el-ti**yoor** el-istinā'**ee**ya | هل عندكم الرماية على الطيور الاصطناعية؟ |
| Is there a rifle range near? | **feeh** maidān lil-re**mā**ya **grey**yib | هل يوجد ميدان للرماية قريب؟ |

Vocabulary

backsight	sid**dā**da khalf**ee**ya	سدادة خلفية
barrel	mā**soo**ret bunde**gee**ya	ماسورة بندقية
bullets	ru**sās**	رصاص
butt	mig**badh**	مقبض البندقية
cartridges	khar**too**sha	خرطوشة
catch	**shab**ka	شبك
ejector	**tā**rid [**gā**dhif]	طارد [قاذف]
foresight	dhib**bā**na	ذبانة
hammer	deek el-bunde**gee**ya [**ze**mur]	ديك البندقية [زمر]
revolver	mu**sed**des	مسدس
safety catch	e**mān**	امان
trigger	zend	زند
telescopic sight	mih**dāf** teles**kou**by	مهداف تلسكوبي

Sailing and Boating

Is there a boat hire agent here?	**yum**kin isti'**jār zou**reg	هل يمكن استئجار زورق؟
I'd like to hire a dinghy/boat.	ebeste'**jir zou**reg sug**heer**/**mar**keb	أريد استأجر زورق صغير/مركب
Is an outboard motor extra?	**feeh uj**ra idhā**fee**ya ala mu**har**rik mue**kh**iret el-**zou**reg	هل لمحرك مؤخرة الزورق اجرة اضافية؟
Does this have an auxiliary engine?	**feeh** mu**har**rik idhā**fee**ya li-**hā**dha	هل يوجد محرك اضافي لهذا؟

How many berths are there?	**kem** sereer **fee**ha	كم سرير فيها؟
How much water does it draw?	ish-**meda gh**ātus el-se**fee**na	ما مدى غاطس السفينة؟
Is there a stove/sink/ chemical toilet?	**feeh** **fir**in/houdh el-**ma**/tuw**ā**lait keemy**ā**eeya	هل يوجد فرن/حوض الماء/ توااليت كيميائية؟
Does it include cutlery, china and cooking utensils?	**yesh**mil **hā**dha kill el-**fudhee**ya, **seeny** wa edew**āt** el-**ta**bukh	هل هذا يشمل كل الفضية صيني وأدوات الطبخ؟
Have you got a map of the river?	**in**dek khar**ee**tet el-**na**her	هل عندك خريطة النهر؟
How far is it to the next place where I can get some fuel?	**wain** egrab me**hat**tet ben**zeen**	أين أقرب محطة بنزين؟
Can I leave the boat here while we go to the shops?	**mum**kin ekhally el-**zoureg** hina wa ana **rā**yih lil-**soog**	ممكن اترك الزورق هنا بينما نذهب للسوق؟
Where is the next refuse dump?	**wain** fee **miz**bela **grey**yiba	أين أقرب مزبلة؟
Will you please give me a tow?	**mum**kin te**jur**rny jerr	ممكن تجرني جرا؟

Vocabulary

anchor	**mer**sa [**len**gar]	مرساة
boat	**mer**kab	مركب
boathook	ug**ā**fa	عقافة
canoe	**zoureg** bi**doon** shrā' [**belem**]	زورق بدون شراع
chart	khar**ee**ta bah**ree**ya	خريطة بحرية
deck	**dha**her el-se**fee**na	ظهر السفينة

diesel engine	muharrik **dee**zel	محرك ديزل
dinghy	zu**wai**rag	زويرق
fender	**mi**sadd	مصد
halyard	habl el-sherā'	حبل الشراع
hull	**hai**kel el-se**fee**na	هيكل السفينة
jib	sherā' e**mām**y	شراع أمامي
keel	gā'idet el-se**fee**na	قاعدة السفينة
leak	**tha**gub [shegg]	ثقب [شق]
lifebelt	hizām el-ne**jāt**	حزام النجاة
lifejacket	si**dār** el-ne**jāt**	صدار النجاة
mainsail	sherā' **khal**fy	شراع خلفي
mast	**sār**y	صاري
motorboat	lensh	مركب بموتور
oar/paddle	mij**dhāf**	مجذاف
outboard motor	mu**har**rik bimu**wek**her el-**zou**reg	محرك بمؤخر الزورق
pennant	**rā**ya [**bai**rag]	راية [بيرق]
port (left)	yi**sār**	يسار
propeller	ru**fās**	رفاص
rowing boat	**mar**keb bi-mejā**dheef**	مركب بمجاذيف
sail	sherā'	شراع
shallow	ghair a**meeg**	غير عميق
starboard (right)	ye**meen**	يمين
steering	gi**yā**da [tou**jeeh**]	قيادة [توجيه]
stern	mu**wek**heret el-se**fee**na	مؤخرة السفينة
storm	**ā**sifa	عاصفة
tiller	dhirā' el-gārib	ذراع القارب
wind	reeh	ريح
yacht	**mar**keb [**yak**hit]	مركب [يخت]

General Services

If you are travelling independently or taking over a self-catering villa or apartment, phrases for dealing with gas, electricity and plumbing problems will be indispensable. But even when all that is taken care of by someone else it is useful to be able to communicate with Post Office staff, telephone operators and other officials in their own language.

Post Office

Is there a Post Office near here?	feeh be**reed greyy**ib	هل يوجد بريد قريب من هنا؟
What are the opening hours?	**shin**-hy oug**āt** el-amel	ما هي أوقات العمل؟
Can I cash an international money order here?	**mum**kin a**s**rif huw**āla māleeya** dou**leeya** hina	ممكن أصرف حوالة مالية دولية هنا؟
I want some stamps for a letter to Britain.	eby tow**ābi' be**reed ila breet**ā**nya	أريد طوابع بريدية إلى بريطانيا.
What is the postcard postage rate for the USA?	bi**kem** el-but**āga** ila emreeka	كم ثمن طابع بطاقة بريدية إلى أمريكا؟
I'd like to register this letter.	eby asejjil **hā**dhy el-ris**āla**	أحب أن أسجل هذه الرسالة.
I want to send it airmail. express. by surface rate. by printed matter rate.	eby ersilha bil-be**reed** el**jowy** musta'jila dereja th**ān**ya ujret matboo'**āt**	أريد أن أرسلها بالبريد الجوي. مستعجلة. درجة ثانية. أجرة المطبوعات.
Where do I post parcels?	wain a**weddy** el-tu**rood**	أين أضع الطرود؟

Do I need a customs form?	yibghā-la istimāret jumruk	هل أحتاج إستمارة؟
Is there a poste restante here?	feeh mekteb li-hafudh hina	هل يوجد مكتب لحفظ هنا؟
Have you a letter for me?	feeh risāla ly	هل لي رسالة؟
May I have a telegram form?	min fadhlek eby nemoodhej bergiyya	من فضلك أريد نموذج برقية.
I'll send it by the cheap rate/normal rate.	ersilha dereja thānya/ādeeya	سأرسلها درجة ثانية / عادية.
When will it arrive?	mita yāsil	متى ستصل؟
I want to make a telephone call. an international call. a person to person call.	eby a'mel mukālema tilaifooneeya mukālema douleeya mukālema shakhseeya	أريد أن أعمل مكالمة هاتفية دولية شخصية.
Can you reverse the charges?	mumkin yidfa' el-jānib el-thāny	هل يمكن أن تسجل أجرة المكالمة؟
Switchboard, the line is engaged. Please try again later.	el-khatt meshghool. min fadhlek hāwil ba'ad shweyya	الخط مشغول. من فضلك حاول بعد قليل.

The Police Station

| Where is the police station? | wain merkez el-shurta | أين مركز الشرطة؟ |
| I would like to report a theft/loss/ accident/crime. | eby akhbirkum 'an seriga/hādith/shai dhāyi'/jereema | أريد أن أبلغ عن سرقة / حادث / شيء ضائع / جريمة. |

Someone stole my wallet.	**sir**get maha**fidh**ety [in**bāg**et maha**fidh**ety]	سرقت محفظتي.
Something was stolen from my car/my hotel room.	**sir**ig [in**bāg**] shai min seyy**ā**rety/min **ghur**fety bil**fin**dug	سرق شيء من سيارتي / غرفتي بالفندق
The theft occurred in the . . . at about four o'clock.	**had**ethet el-**ser**iga fy . . . how**ā**lai el-s**ā**'a **er**ba'a	حدث السرقة في... حوالي الساعة الرابعة.
I have lost my watch on the beach.	dhayy**a't** s**ā**'ety yemm el-**ba**her	ضيعت ساعتي على الشاطى
It is valuable.	hiya gh**ā**leeya	إنها غالية.
It has sentimental value.	h**ā**dha shai a**zeez** indy	لها ذكرة عزيزة.
I will offer a reward.	eby a**ged**dim muk**ā**fa'a	سأقدم مكافأة.
Someone has been knocked down.	indi'am w**ā**hid	طرح أرضا.
A lady has broken her leg.	feeh **sey**yida in**kis**eret **rij**ilha	سيدة كسرت رجلها.
I have been swindled.	gheshsh**ou**ny	خدعوني.
Can a police officer come with me?	**mum**kin yer**ā**figny dh**ā**bit boul**ees**	ممكن ضابط بوليس يرافقني؟
I will be a witness.	ana e**koon** sh**ā**hid	سأكون شاهدا.
I cannot be a witness. I did not see what was happening.	m**ā** **eg**dar e**koon** sh**ā**hid. m**ā** shift el-**hā**ditha	لا أستطيع أن أكون شاهدا. لم أر ما حدث.
Is there anyone who speaks English?	feeh **ah**ed yite**kel**lem ing**la**izy	هل هناك من يتكلم الانجليزية؟

Electricity

The lights have gone out.	intufet el-adhwā	أنطفت الأضواء.
The power plug is not working.	el-blek atlāna	الفيشة عطلانة.
The fuse has gone.	el-fyooz maharooga	الفيوز محروقة.
I think it's the switch.	edhunn el-atal bil-sweech	أظن أنه السوتش.
There is a smell of burning.	reehet hareega	ريحة حريقة.
The stove won't light.	mā yishtighil el-firen	الموقد لن يعمل.
The heating has broken down.	inguta‘at el-tedfeeya	إنقطعت التدفئة.
Can you mend it straight away?	mumkin tisallih-ha bisur‘a	ممكن تصلحها. بسرعة؟
Where is the fuse box?	wain mahell el-fyoozāt	أين العداد الكهربائي؟
Which is the main switch?	wain el-miftāh el-re'eesy	أين المفتاح الرئيسي؟

VOCABULARY

adaptor	muhowwil	محول
bulb	lemba	لمبة.
electric cooker	firen kaharubāee	غاز كهربائي.
electric fire	midfa‘a kaharubāeeya	مدفأة كهربائية.
extension lead	touseelāt	توصيلات.
fuse wire	silk el-fyooz	فيوز.
hair dryer	seshwār	مجفف الشعر.
insulating tape	shereet ‘āzil	شريط عازل.
iron	mikwa	حديد
plug	belouk	بلوك

radio	**rād**yo	راديو
refrigerator	thel**lāj**a	ثلاجة
television	tilifiz**yoon**	تلفزيون
torch	ba**tār**ya	بطارية [كهربا]
water heater	mu**sakh**in el-ma	مسخن الماء

Gas

There is a smell of gas.	feeh **ree**het ghāz	هناك رائحة غاز.
It must be a gas leak.	**lāz**im feeh te**serr**ub ghāz	لازم يكون فيه تسرب غاز.
This is the gas meter.	**hādh**y ad**dād** el-ghāz	هذا عداد الغاز.
This gas jet won't light.	**mā yish**ti'il **hādh**a	هذا الأنبوب الغاز لايشتعل.
The pilot light keeps going out.	el-mis**bāh** at**lān**	المصباح معطل.
Is there any danger of an explosion?	feeh **khat**ar infi**jār**	هل هناك خطر انفجار؟
I think the ventilator is blocked.	ed**hunn** me**jra** el-**how**a mes**dood**	أعتقد أن المكيف مسدود.
We can't get any hot water.	**mā** tijy **māy sākh**in	لا نستطيع الحصول على ماء ساخن.

VOCABULARY

chimney	**mid**khana	مدخنة
gas fire	**mid**fa'a	مدفأة
gas light	dhou ghāz	ضوء غاز
gas pipe	en**boob** ghāz	أنبوب غاز
gas tap	hane**fee**yet ghāz	حنفية غاز
geyser	**gai**zer	جيزر
hammer	mut**riga** [shā**koosh**]	مطرقة [شاكوش]
key	mif**tāh**	مفتاح

lagging	**mād**da āzila [**teghleef**]	مادة عازلة [تغليف]
spanner	mif**tāh ra**but	مفتاح ربط
water heater	mu**sak**hin **el**-mā	مسخن الماء

Plumbing

Are you the plumber?	ent el-seb**bāk**	هل أنت السباك ؟
The sink is stopped up.	houdh **el**-ma mes**dood**	حوض الماء مسدود
There is a blockage in the pipe.	el-en**boob** mes**dood**	الأنبوب مسدود
The tap needs a new washer.	el-hane**fee**ya teby **hal**ga ji**dee**da	الحنفية تحتاج إلى حلقة جديدة
This water pipe is leaking.	en**boob** el-mā **hā**dha te**her**rib **mā**	أنبوب الماء يخر.
The lavatory cistern won't fill.	el-see**foun** at**lān**	السيفون عطلان.
The valve is stuck.	el-su**mām** mu**hab**bes	الصمام محبس
The float is punctured.	el-a**wā**ma makh**roo**ma	العوامة مخرومة
The water tank has run dry.	el-khez**zān mā** bah **mā**	الخزان ما به ماء
The tank is overflowing.	**fādh** el-khez**zān**	فاض الخزان

Vocabulary

basin	**magh**sela	مغسلة
bath	**bān**yo	حمام/بانيو
cesspool	ba**loo**‘a	بالوعة
immersion heater	mu**sek**hin **ghā**tus	مسخن غاطس

main drainage	enboob el-tasreef el-re'eesy	انبوب التصريف الرئيسي
mains water	enboob el-mā el-re'eesy	انبوب الماء الرئيسي
overflow pipe	enboob fāyidh	انبوب فائض
plug	belouk	بلوك
stopcock	mehbes [hanefeeyet wagf el-tedeffug]	محبس [حنفية وقف التدفق]

Personal Services

This section suggests useful phrases for such occasions as a visit to a doctor, dentist, hairdresser, hospital or beautician.

At the Doctor's

Can you recommend a doctor?	**mum**kin tin**sah**ny bi-tu**beeb**	ممكن تنصحني بطبيب؟
Is there an English-speaking doctor in the town?	**feeh** tu**beeb** yite**kellem** in**glaizy** bil-wu**lāya**	هل هناك طبيب يتكلم انجليزي في البلدة؟
Where is the surgery?	**wain** el-i**yāda**	أين العيادة؟
I have an appointment. My name is . . .	**indy** mou**'id. ismy** . . .	عندي ميعاد. اسمي...
Can the doctor come to the hotel/house?	**mum**kin el-duk**toor** yijy lil-**fin**dug/lil-**bait**	ممكن الدكتور يحضر إلى الفندق/البيت؟
I'm not feeling well.	ana ta**bān** [**māny** bel**hail**]	انا تعبان
I feel sick/dizzy/ shivery/faint.	ana ma**reedh**/**dāyikh**/ **indy** ra**'sha**/**indy** dhu**'ef**	انا مريض/دائخ/برعشة/بضعف.
The pain is here.	el-**wuja'** hina	الوجع هنا.
I have hurt my . . .	**indy wuja'** fy el . . .	عندي ألم في الـ....
I have a temperature. a headache. back ache. sore throat. sunburn.	**indy** ha**rāra** su**dā'** **wuja'** fy el-**dhaher** **wuja'** fy el-han**joor** **hareg** min el-shems	عندي حرارة صداع ألم في الظهر ألم في الحلق حرق من الشمس

I have diarrhoea.	indy is-hāl	عندي إسهال
I am constipated.	indy imsāk	عندي إمساك
I have been vomiting.	ana ezouwa'	عندي قيء
I have been like this since yesterday.	esh'ur bihādha el-wuja' min ems	اشعر بهذا الالم منذ امس
Do you want me to undress?	enza' hudoomy	هل اخلع ملابسي؟
Is it serious?	el-hāla khuteera	هل الحالة خطيرة؟
Should I stay in bed?	lāzim ebga bil-ferāsh	هل الزم الفراش؟
Should I arrange to go home?	mumkin erja' lil-bait.	هل استعد للعودة إلى البيت؟
I am allergic to . . .	indy hassāseeya dhidd . . .	عندي حساسية ضد...
I have a heart condition.	indy maradh el-galb	عندي مرض القلب
I am asthmatic/diabetic.	indy dheeg el-nefes/maradh el-sukker	عندي مرض الربو/ مرض السكر
I am pregnant.	ana hamil	انا حامل
Do I have to pay for hospitalization and medicines?	lāzim edfa' tekāleef el-musteshfa wa el-edwiya	هل على ان ادفع تكاليف المستشفى والأدوية؟
It's only a slight problem.	el-mushkila buseeta	المشكل بسيط جدا

VOCABULARY

PARTS OF THE BODY

ankle	gusubet el-rijil	قصبة الرجل
appendix	el-musrān el-awer	المصران الاعور
arm	dhirā' [yed]	ذراع
artery	sheryān	شريان
back	dhaher	ظهر
bladder	methāna	مثانة
blood	dem	دم
bone	adhum	عظم
bowels	em'ā [aheshā]	أمعاء [احشاء]
breast	thedy [nehaid]	ثدي
cheek	khed	خد
chest	sadur	صدر
chin	hanek [hanich]	ذقن
collarbone	turguwwa	ترقوة
ear	idhin	اذن
elbow	koo'	كوع
eye	ain	عين
face	wejeh	وجه
finger	usbu'	أصبع
foot	gadem [rijil]	قدم
forehead	jebeen	جبين
gland	ghudda	غدة
hand	yed [eed]	يد
heart	galb	قلب
heel	ka'ab [cha'ab]	كعب
hip	ridf	ردف
intestine	mesāreen/mehāry	مصارين
jaw	fekk [fech]	فك [لحي]
joint	mifsal	مفصل
kidney	kilwa [chilwa]	كلية
knee	rukba	ركبة
leg	sāg [rijil]	ساق
lip	shifa [burtum]	شفة

liver	kebd [chebd]	كبد
lung	**riya**	رئة
mouth	fem [them, halg]	فم
muscle	adhul	عضل
neck	ruguba	رقبة
nerve	aseb	عصب
nose	enf [**khashim**]	انف
penis	gud**heeb** [zibb, air]	قضيب [الة الرجل]
rib	dhule'	ضلع
shoulder	kitf [chitf]	كتف
skin	jild	جلد
spine	el-a**mood** el-**fa**gery	العمود الفقري
stomach	**mi**'da	معدة
tendon	ar**goob**	عرقوب
testicle	khus**yän**	خصية
thigh	fakhidh	فخذ
throat	han**joor**	الزور [الزلاعيم]
thumb	ib**häm**	ابهام
toe	usbu' el-**ri**jil	اصبع الرجل
tongue	lis**än**	لسان
tonsils	louz	لوز
urine	boul	بول
vagina	**mih**bel [**fa**rej]	مهبل
vein	areg	عرق
womb	**ra**him	رحم
wrist	**mi**'sam	معصم

INDISPOSITIONS

abscess	**di**mil	دمل
asthma	rabuw [dheeg el-**ne**fes]	ربو
bite (dog/insect)	adhet [**kelb**, **ha**shera]	قرصت [حشرة]
blisters	**naf**ta	نفطة
boil	khu**räj**	خراج
burn/scald	**ha**reg	حرق
chill	**ba**red	برد
cold	zu**käm**	زكام

convulsions	teshennujāt	تشنجات
cut	gatu' [jareh]	قطع [جرح]
diabetes	maredh el-sukker	مرض السكر
diarrhoea	is-hāl	إسهال
dizziness	doukha	دوخة
haemorrhoids	buwāseer	بواسير
hay fever	zukām rabee'y	زكام ربيعي
indigestion	asur hadhum	عسر هضم
infection	isāba	اصابة
inflammation	iltihāb	التهاب
influenza	inflooenza	انفلونزا
irritation	hareg [hakka]	حرق
nausea	ghishyān	غشيان
rash	tafuh jildy	طفح جلدي
rheumatism	roomatizm	روماتيزم
shivers	ra'sha	رعشة
stiff neck	iltiwā fy el-unug	التواء في العنق
sting	ledugh	لدغ
sunstroke	dharbet shems	ضربة شمس
tonsillitis	iltihāb fy el-zour	التهاب في الزور
ulcer	gurha	قرحة
whooping cough	su'āl deeky	سعال ديكي
wound	jareh	جرح

At the Dentist's

Can you recommend a dentist?	mumkin te'arrifny ala tubeeb esnān	ممكن تعرفني على طبيب أسنان؟
I need an appointment as soon as possible.	eby mou'idin ājil	اريد موعدا عاجلا
I have a toothache/an abscess.	indy wuja' el-esnān/khurāj	عندي ألم في اسناني/خراج
I've lost a filling.	tāh hashw el-sinn	سقط حشو السن

Can you suggest a painkiller to take in the meantime?	**mum**kin tu'**teeny** mu**khed**ir fy el-wagt el-**hā**ly	ممكن تعطيني مخدراً في الوقت الحالي
The bad tooth is at the front/back.	el-**wuja'** fy el-esn**ān** el-emā**mee**ya/el-khal**fee**ya	الألم في الأسنان الأمامية/الخلفية
Can you extract it?	**mum**kin tekhla'-ha	ممكن تخلعها؟
Does it need a filling?	teby **hash**wa	تحتاج حشوة؟
Can you put in a temporary filling?	**mum**kin tehutt **hesh**wa mu**wag**geta	هل ممكن تضع حشوة موقتة؟
Can I eat normally?	**mum**kin ākil bir**āha**	ممكن آكل براحة؟
I'd prefer gas to an injection.	e**fadhil** el-**benj** ala el-**ibra**	افضل البنج على الابرة.
My gums are bleeding.	el-**letha** ten**zif**	اللثة تنزف
I have broken my dentures.	ki**sert tagmy**	كسرت طقمي.
What is your fee?	**bikem** el-kesh**fee**ya	كم الكشفية؟

At the Optician's

Can you recommend an optician?	**mum**kin te'**arrif**ny ala tu**beeb** el-**ain**	ممكن تعرفني على طبيب العين؟
I have broken my glasses.	ki**sert** men**ādh**ery	كسرت نظارتي.
Can you repair them temporarily?	**yum**kin tu**sall**iha mu**wag**geten	هل يمكنك اصلاحها موقتا؟
The lens is broken. Can you get a new one quickly?	el-**ad**isa mek**soo**ra. **mum**kin te**hass**il ala **wāh**ida je**dee**da bisur'a	العدسة مكسورة. ممكن احصل على واحدة جديدة بسرعة؟
Have you got contact lenses?	**in**dek adis**āt lā**siga	هل عندك عدسات لاصقة؟

I'd like a pair of tinted spectacles.	eby nedhārāt ghāmiga	اريد نظارات غامقة.
Do you sell binoculars/ sunglasses?	hel tebee' mukebbirāt/nedhārāt shemseeya	هل تبيع مكبرات/نظارات شمسية؟
I had better have an eye test.	eby fahes nadher	اريد فحص نظر
I am short-sighted/ long-sighted.	ana indy gusr el-nadher/ tool el-nadher	انا عندي قصر النظر/ طول النظر
How long will it take for my new glasses to be ready?	mita tehadhar el-nedhārāt el-jedeeda	متى تحضر النظارات الجديدة؟
How much will they cost?	kem tikellif	كم ستكلف؟

At the Chiropodist's

I have a painful corn.	indy kālo yooji'ny	عندي كالو يؤلمني
Can you remove it?	mumkin tezeela	ممكن تزيله؟
I have a bunion which is rubbing against my shoe.	indy warem yooji'a el-gandera	عندي ورم يحك في الحذاء.
I have a hard spot on the ball of my foot.	indy khurra hader ibhām el-gadem	عندي خرة تحت ابهام القدم
My nails need attention. One of them is ingrowing.	edhāfiry teby ināya. wāhid minha nāmyin ila el-dākhil	أظافري محتاجة لعناية. واحد منها نام إلى الداخل.
Have you anything to soften them?	indek shai li-terteeb el-edhāfir	هل عندك شيء لترطيب الأظافر؟
The soles of my feet are very sore.	bātin egdāmy yooji'ny shedeed	باطن اقدامي يؤلمني كثيرا.

At the Hairdresser's

Where is the nearest hairdresser? Is there one in the hotel?	**wain** egrab **sāloun** el-tejmeel. **feeh** wāhid fy el-**fin**dug	أين اقرب صالون التجميل؟ هل يوجد واحد في الفندق؟
I'd like to make an appointment.	eby **mou'id**	أريد موعداً.
I want a cut and set/a shampoo and set.	eby **gass** u tes**reeh**/**shām**bo wa tes**reeh**	أريد قص وتسريح / شامبو وتسريح
I wear it brushed forward with a fringe.	im**shut** sha'ry ila jid**dām**	أمشط شعري إلى الأمام
I like it brushed back.	im**shu**ta ila el-**wa**ra min **fadh**lek	أمشطه إلى الوراء من فضلك.
Can you please put some waves/curls in?	**mum**kin tud**ri**ja/tehutt bouk**lāt**	ممكن تدرجه/ تحط بوكلات
Draw it back into a bun.	im**shu**ta sheen**you**n ila el-**wa**ra	أمشطه شينيون إلى الوراء.
Give me a colour rinse, please.	eby ghe**seel** bil-**loun** min **fadh**lek	أريد غسيل باللون من فضلك.
I think I will have it dyed.	eby su**bā**gha	أريد صباغة.
Have you got a colour chart?	**in**dek de**leel** el-el**wān**	هل عندك دليل الألوان؟
No hairspray, thank you.	be**lā**shin min el-s**brāy**	بلا سبراي من فضلك.
I'd like a manicure.	eby mānee**keer**	أريد مانيكير.
What is the name of this varnish?	**shism** mulem**mi'** el-e**dhā**fir **hā**dha	ما اسم ملمع الأظافر هذا؟

Vocabulary

auburn	**bun**ny	بنى
blonde	**esh**gar·	أشقر
brunette	**es**wed	أسود
comb	**mi**shut	مشط
dryer	mu**jeff**if	مجفف
ginger	**a**hamar	أحمر
hairnet	**she**beket el-sha'r	شبكة الشعر
hair pin	fer**shee**net el-sha'r	فرشينة الشعر
scissors	mi**gass**	مقص
styling	**mou**dha [tej**meel**]	موضة [تجميل]
razor	**moo**sa	موس
rollers	le**fā**yif lil-tem**weej**	لفائف للتمويج

At the Beauty Salon

I'd like	eby	لريد
a complete beauty treatment.	tej**meel kā**mil min **fadh**lek	تجميل كامل من فضلك.
just a facial.	el-**we**jeh **fa**gat	الوجه فقط
to change my make-up	tegh**yeer** el-**māk**yāj	تغيير المكياج
something more suitable for the seaside.	shai **es**lah lil-**ba**her	شيء مناسب اكثر للبحر
something lighter in tone.	shai **lou**na ef**tah**	لون افتح
something for the evening.	shaî lil-**seh**ra	للسهرة
I have a delicate skin.	**jil**dy re**geeg**	جلدي رقيق
Can you please suggest a new eye make-up?	**mum**kin tansi**hee**ny bimāk**yāj** je**deed**	ممكن تنصحيني بماكياج جديد للعيون؟
I think that is too heavy.	ed**hunn hā**dha the**geel ek**thar min el-**lā**zim	أظن هذا ثقيل اكثر من اللازم

Have you any false eyelashes?	**in**dek ru**moosh** istina**'ee**ya	هل عندك رموش اصطناعية؟
Perhaps my eyebrows need plucking.	edhunn he**wā**jiby teby tel**geet**	أظن حواجبي تحتاج تلقيط
I'd like to see some new lipstick colours.	eba**shoof** el**wān rooj** lil-she**fāy**if	أريد أن أرى ألوان روج للشفايف

At the Laundry/Cleaner's

I'd like them washed/cleaned/pressed.	eby ghusl el-me**lā**bis **hā**dhy/tend**heef**/**kow**y	أريد غسل هذه الملابس / تنظيف/كوى من فضلك.
Will this stain come out?	**mum**kin i**zā**let **hā**dhy el-**bag**'a	هل يمكن إزالة هذه البقعة؟
It is a coffee/blood/grease/biro stain.	**hā**dhy bag'et **gah**wa/**dem**/**di**hin/**hi**ber	هذه بقعة قهوة/دم/دهن/ حبر
Will you iron these shirts?	**mum**kin **tek**wy **hā**dhy el-gum**sān**	ممكن تكوى هذه القمصان؟
I will collect them tomorrow.	**ā**khidh**ha bukra**	سآخذها بكرة
Do you deliver?	feeh khidma menze**lee**ya	هل لديكم خدمة منزلية؟
Do you do mending?	**in**dekum **ra**fa	هل عندكم رفة؟
This tear needs patching.	**hā**dha yeby ter**gee'**	هذا يحتاج إلى ترقيع
Can you sew this button on?	**mum**kin te**rak**kib **hā**dhy el-**zirr** [**deg**ma]	ممكن تركب هذه الزر؟
Can you mend this invisibly?	**yim**kin **ra**fat **hā**dha **doon** en **yadh**har	هل يمكن رفة هذا دون أن يظهر؟
This is not my blouse/coat/dress.	**hā**dha **ma**hoob gu**mee**sy/mi**'ta**fy/fus**tā**ny	هذا ليس قميصي/ معطفي/ فستاني.

My trousers are missing.	**nā**gus el-benta**loun**	ناقص البنطلون.
This was not torn when I brought it to you.	**hā**dha **mā** kān mu**mezz**eg **lem**man sel**lem**ta **li**kum	هذا لم يكن ممزق عندما سلمته اليكم.
How long does the launderette stay open?	**mi**ta tu**'ezz**il el-**magh**sela	متى تغلق المغسلة؟

VOCABULARY

bleach	mah**lool** el-teb**yeedh**	محلول التبييض
cleaning fluid	mu**na**dhif	منظف
clothes hanger	al**lā**ga [shem**mā**'a]	علاقة [شماعة]
dryer	mu**jeff**if el-me**lā**bis	مجفف الملابس
launderette	me**hall** ghe**seel** el-thi**yāb**	محل غسيل الثياب
rinse	**shat**ef	شطف
soap powder	**sā**boon	صابون
washing machine	ghes**sā**la kahrub**āee**ya	غسالة كهربائية
water	mā	ماء
hot/warm/cold	**sā**khin/**dā**fy/**bā**rid	ساخن/داف/بارد

At the Men's Hairdresser's

I want a haircut, please.	eby **khaff**a min **fadh**lek	اريد قص شعر من فضلك.
Just a trim, please. I haven't much time.	**khaff**a bu**see**ta min **fadh**lek. ana musta'jil	قص بسيط من فضلك انا مستعجل.
Please give me a shampoo.	eby **shām**bo min **fadh**lek	اريد شامبو من فضلك.
I would like it cut shorter.	**gus**sa **ag**sar	قصه اقصر
Leave it long, please.	i**tru**ka tu**weel** min **fadh**lek	اتركه طويل من فضلك.
You are taking too much off.	lā te**guss** ke**theer**	لا تقص كثيرا

Take a little more off the back/sides/top.	guss **ek**thar min el-**khalf**/el-je**wā**nib/ **a'**la	قص اكثر من الخلف/ الجوانب/ أعلى
I part my hair on the left/right.	**ef**rig **sha'**ry ala el-**ji**ha el-**yus**ra/el-**yum**na	أفرق شعري على الجهة اليسرى/اليمنى.
Please give me a shave.	eby teha**leeg** min **fadh**lek	من فضلك إحلقلي.
Could you trim my beard/ moustache/ sideboards?	e**beek** te**hedh**dhib el-**lih**ya/el-she**wā**rib/ el-se**wā**lif	ممكن تهذب لحيتي/ شواربي/ سوالفي؟
No, thank you. I do not want a facial massage.	lā **shuk**ren. **mā** eby ted**leek** el-**we**jeh	لا . شكرا . لا أريد . تدليك وجهي .
I will have a manicure.	eby māne**ekoor**	أريد مانيكير.
May I have a hand towel?	**mum**kin te'a**teen**y **min**shefa	ممكن تعطيني منشفة؟
Put some eau de cologne on but no cream.	hutt kou**loun lā**kin **mā** eby kreem	حط كولونيا. بلاش كريم.
Move the mirror a bit more to the right/left.	**how**wil el-mi**rā**ya **shwey**ya ila el-ye**meen**/ila el-shi**māl**	حرك المراة شوية إلى اليمين/ إلى الشمال.
Yes, that's fine.	**ai**wa, a**dheem**	أيوه ، عظيم!

Making Friends

Good morning.	sabāh el-khair	صباح الخير.
Good afternoon [good evening].	mesā el-khair	مساء الخير.
May I introduce my friend John/my wife?	e'arrif sudeegy jon/zoujety	أعرفك على صديقي جون/زوجتي.
My name is . . .	ismy . . .	إسمي...
How do you do?	ehlen wa sehlen	أهلا وسهلا.
Are you staying at this hotel/at this resort?	ent nāzil bihādha el-findug/fy hādha el-maseef	أنت نازل بهذا الفندق/ في هذا المصيف؟
Are you enjoying your holiday?	ent mistānis hina	هل أنت مستمتع بعطلتك؟
How long have you been on holiday?	kem youm sār lek bil-'utla	من متى أخذت عطلة؟
Do you always come here?	tijy hina dāymen	هل تجيء هنا دائما؟
I'd like you to meet my friend . . .	ebeek tegābil sudeegy . . .	أريدك أن تقابل صديقي...
Would you care to have a drink with us?	teby tishreb shai ma'na	تريد أن تشرب شيئا معنا؟
What would you like?	ish-teby	ماذا تريد؟
Please, I insist that you let me.	ebden! khalleeny edfa'	أرجوك ، خليني أدفع.
I don't speak Arabic very well.	mā etekellem areby killish zain	أنا لا أتكلم العربية جيدا.

It is very nice to talk to an Arab person.	yesherrifny ekellim wāhid areby	انا يشرفني أن اتكلم مع عربي.
Which part of the Middle East do you come from?	ent aslek wain fy el-sharg el-ousat	أنت جايي من اي منطقة في الشرق الأوسط؟
I am here with my wife/husband/family/friends.	ana hina ma' zoujety/zoujy/āyilty/asdigāy	انا هنا مع زوجتي/ زوجي/ عائلتي/ أصدقاء.
Are you alone?	ent bwahdek	أنت لوحدك؟
We come from England.	hinna jāyyeen min ingiltera	نحن من أنجلترا.
Have you been to England?	jeet ingiltera ent	أنت رحت أنجلترا؟
If you come, please let me know.	khabbirny min fadhlek idha jeet	خبرني من فضلك إذا جئت.
This is my address.	hādha inwāny	هذا عنواني.
I hope to see you again soon.	inshalla eshoofek gareeben	أتمنى أن أراك قريبا.
Perhaps we could meet for a drink after dinner?	rubbema nishreb shai ba'd el-'asha	ربما نشرب شيئا بعد العشاء؟
I should be delighted to join you.	yessurreny jidden en erāfigek	يسعدني جدا أن أرافقك.
At what time shall I come?	mita ejy	متى آجي؟
Have you got any children?	indek oulād	هل عندك عائلة؟
Would you like to see some photos of our house and our children?	tehibb teshoof suwer el-bait wa el-oulād	تحب أن ترى بعض صور البيت والأطفال؟

Are you going to the gala?	ent **rāyih** el-**hafla**	أنت ذاهب للحفلة؟
Would you like us to go together?	tehibb nerooh hinna wiyyākum	هل تحب أن نذهب مع بعض؟
It has been very nice to meet you.	tesharrefna	تشرفنا بمقابلتك.
You have been very kind.	alla ykeththir khairek	أشكرك على لطفك.

Dating Someone

Note. The phrases in round brackets in the phonetics are the ones you should use if talking to a girl.

Are you on holiday?	hādhy 'utletek (hādhy 'utletich)	أنت معطل [معطلة]؟
Do you live here?	ent sākin hina (enty sākina hina)	أنت ساكن [ساكنة] هنا؟
Do you like this place?	ent mistānis (enty mistānisa) fy hādha el-mukān	مبسوط [مبسوطة] في هذا المكان؟
I've just arrived.	towwy wusilt	وصلت الآن.
What is there to do?	ai khidma	اي خدمة؟
I don't know anyone here.	mā a'arif ahed hina	لا أعرف أحدا هنا.
I'm with a group of students.	ana ma' majmoo'tin min el-tullāb	أنا مع مجموعة من الطلاب.
I'm travelling alone.	ana musāfir liwahdy	أنا مسافر لوحدي.
I'm on my way to Europe.	ana fy tureegy ila oorubba	انا في طريقي إلى أوروبا.
I come from Scotland/ Australia/ New Zealand.	ana min iskotlenda/ ustrālya/ nyoozeelenda	أنا من اسكتلندا/ أستراليا/ نيوزلندة.

Do you mind if I speak Arabic with you?	mumkin etekellem ma‘ek (ma‘ich) areby	ممكن أحكي معك عربي؟
My Arabic is not very good.	lughety el arebeeya mā heeb guwiyya	عربيتي غير ممتازة.
Would you like a drink?	teby tishreb shai (tebeen tishrebeen shai)	هل تحب أن تشرب شيئا؟
What are you doing this evening?	ish-tisowwy (ish-tisowween) el-‘asr el-youm	ماذا ستفعل هذا المساء؟
Would you like to	tehibb tijy (tehibbeen tijeen)	هل تحبين أن
go to a discotheque?	ila deesko	تذهبي إلى ديسكو؟
join our party?	tijy (tijeen) ma‘na	تجي إلى حفلتنا؟
Do you like dancing?	tehibb (tehibbeen) el-ragus	تحبي الرقص؟
Can I walk along with you?	mumkin etemesha ma‘ek (ma‘ich)	ممكن أمشي معك؟
Which way are you going?	ai soub teby terooh (tebeen terooheen)	أي طريق تذهبين؟
Do you mind if I sit here?	mumkin ag‘ed hina	ممكن أقعد هنا؟
This is my friend, Tom.	hādha sudeegy tom	هذا صديقي ، توم.
Do you have a girl friend?	indek refeega	هل عندك صديقة؟
We could make a foursome.	yimkin nijtima‘ arbe‘atna	يمكن نجتمع أربعة.
Do you play tennis/golf?	til‘ab (til‘abeen) el-tenis/el-goulf	هل تلعب التنس/الجولف؟
Do you go swimming?	tisbah ent (tisbaheen enty)	هل تسبح؟
Which beach do you go to?	ai shāty terooh-la (terooheen-la)	لأي شاطىء تذهب؟

Would you like to come	tehibb terāfigny (tehibbeen terāfigeenny) fy joulatin	هل تحب أن ترافقني في جولة
for a drive/a boat trip?	fy el-seyyāra/fy el-sefeena	في السيارة/في السفينة؟
It would be nice if you would.	ehlen wa sehlen	ما أجمل أن ترافقني.
Thanks for coming out with me.	shukren ala murāfigatek (murāfigatich) liyya	شكرا على مرافقتك لي.
I enjoyed it.	inbusatt [istānest]	انبسطت.
Can we meet again?	mumkin niltigy marra thānya	ممكن نلتقي مرة أخرى؟
How about tomorrow?	mumkin bukra	ممكن بكرة؟
No thanks, I'm busy.	la shukren ana meshghool	لا شكرا أنا مشغول.
Please stop bothering me.	ib'ad anny	أبعد عني من فضلك.

Mutual Interest

Do you play cards?	til'eb wareg	هل تلعب ورق؟
Would you like to make a four at bridge?	mumkin nil'ab li'bet breedj rubā'eeya	هل ممكن تلعب لعبة بريدج رباعية؟
We play canasta/poker/ rummy.	nil'ab kānāsta/bouker/ rāmy	نلعب كاناستا/بوكر/ رامي.
It is an English game.	hādhy li'ba inglaizeeya	هذه لعبة انجليزية.
Are you a chess player?	til'eb el-shatrenj	هل تلعب الشطرنج؟
I'll ask the concierge if the hotel has a chess board.	es'al bouwāb el-houtail an louhet shatrenj	سأسأل بواب الهوتيل عن لوحة الشطرنج.

This is your king/queen/ knight/bishop/ castle/pawn.	**hādha melikek/wezeerek/ faresek/feelek/ gal'atek/askerek**	هذا ملكك/ وزيرك/ فرسك/ فيلك/ قلعتك/ عسكرك.
We could play draughts or dominoes.	**yum**kin nil'ab **dā**ma ou dome**e**no	يمكن ان نلعب داما او دومينو.
We can play table tennis in the hotel. What do you say?	**yim**kin nil'ab tenis el-**tā**wla. wish **rā**yek	يمكن ان نلعب تنس الطاولة في الفندق . ما رايك؟
Do you read English?	**tig**ra ingl**ai**zy	هل تقراء انجليزي.
Would you like to borrow this book/this newspaper?	**teby** tista**'eer** el-ki**tāb hā**dha/ el-je**ree**da **hā**dhy	هل تريد استعارة هذا الكتاب/ هذه الجريدة.

Conversations

There are certain universal subjects of conversation which provide a bridge for communication with strangers all over the world. Among these are the weather, families, home, the cost of living and pets.

The following conversational phrases are designed to start you off on an acquaintanceship with people who do not speak English.

About the Weather

It is a fine day.	el-jou **hi**lu	اليوم جميل
It's not a very nice day.	el-jou **moo** zain [moo bel**hail**]	الجو اليوم بطال.
Will it rain all day/later/ tomorrow?	te**gool** ti**jee**na el-**mut**er ta**wāl** el-ne**hār**/ba'ad **shwai**/**buk**ra	هل ستمطر طوال النهار/ بعد قليل/ غدا؟

It's going to be hot/cold today.	biykoon el-jou hār/bārid el-youm	سيكون الجو حارا/باردا اليوم.
It's rather windy.	feeh howa	هناك الهواء.
I think there is a thunderstorm coming.	edhunn feeh āsifa tijy	أظن هناك عاصفة رعدية.
Look at the lightning.	shuf el-bareg	أنظر البرق
It will soon clear up.	yasfy ba'ad shwai	سيصفي بعد قليل
We don't get this kind of weather at home.	el-jou indena ghair hādha el-jou	الجو عندنا مختلف.
It's a pity it is so dull.	wallah el-dinya ghaim	يا خسارة الجو بطال.
Did you see the beautiful sunrise/sunset?	tuloo'/ghuroob el-shems kān hilu	شروق/غروب الشمس كانت جميلة.
Last year we had a very good/very poor summer.	el-ām kān el-saif jemeel/batāl	العام الماضي كان الصيف جميلا/بطال.
There's a lot of haze about today.	el-youm el-dhubāb wājid	هناك ضباب كثير اليوم.
The atmosphere is very clear.	el-jou sāfy jidden	الهواء صاف جدا.
Is it cold here in the winter?	el-shita bārid hina	هل الشتاء بارد هنا.
I love the spring/summer/autumn.	ehibb el-rebee'/el-saif/ el-khereef	أحب الربيع/الصيف/ الخريف.

VOCABULARY

breeze	neseem	نسيم
cloudburst	rakhet muter	رخة مطر
cloudy	mugheyyem	مغيم

drizzle	**mu**ter khe**feef**	مطر خفيف
dry	**yā**bis	يابس
forecast	te**nebba**	تنبأ
hail	**ba**red	برد
meteorological office	**mas**lahet el-er**sād** el-jou**wee**ya	مصلحة الارصاد الجوية
mist	dhu**bāb**	ضباب
pressure	**dhag**hut	ضغط
rain	**mu**ter	مطر
sleet	shef**shāf**	(مطر فيه ثلج) شفشاف
snow	thelj	ثلج
sunny	mu**shem**mes	مشمس
temperature	**da**rejet el-ha**rā**ra	درجة الحرارة
weather report	el-tenebbu'**āt** el-jou**wee**ya	التنبوءات الجوية

About Families

This is
  my wife/husband/
  daughter/son.
	hādha
	zoujety/**zou**jy **rej**ly/
	binty/**ib**ny
		هذه
		زوجتي/زوجي رجلي/
		بنتي/إبني.

My son is
  an architect/
  doctor/student/
  teacher.
	ibny
	mu**hen**dis/tu**beeb**/
	tālib/mu**der**ris
		إبني
		مهندس/طبيب
		طالب/مدرس.

My daughter is at school.	**bin**ty tedris bil-**med**resa	بنتي تلميذة في المدرسة.
She is taking her examinations.	hiya fy **fet**ret el-imtihā**nāt**	إنها في فترة امتحانات.

Then she will go to
  university.
  teacher's training
  college.
  art school.
	u ba'**dain** terooh
	el-**jā**mi'a
	kul**lee**yet
	el-mu'alli**meen**
	ma'hed el-fu**noon** el-je**mee**la
		ويعد ستذهب إلى
		الجامعة.
		كلية المعلمين
		معهد الفنون الجميلة.

She learned some Arabic at school.	derisat shweyya areby fy el-**medresa**	درست قليلا من اللغة العربية في المدرسة.
My wife is Scottish.	**zouj**ety min iskutlen**da**	زوجتي من اسكتلندا.
My father was a teacher.	e**booy** kān mu‘allim	كان أبي معلما.
The children prefer to have holidays on their own.	el-atfāl yufadhi**loon** yuseyyi**foon** barwāh-hum	الأطفال يفضلون العطلة بمفردهم.
They prefer camping.	yufadhi**loon** el-te**khey**yum	يفضلون التخييم.
My youngest/eldest son is married and lives in . . .	el-weled el-sugheer/ el-kibeer mitzowwij wa sākin fy . . .	أصغر/ أكبر ولد متزوج وساكن في . . .
My youngest/eldest daughter is married and lives in . . .	el-bint el-sugheera/ el-kibeera mitzowwija wa sākina fy . . .	أصغر/ أكبر بنت متزوجة وتعيش في . . .
Would you like to see some photos of our family?	teby te**shoof** ba‘edh el-**suw**er min **āy**letna	هل تريد أن ترى بعض صور عائلتنا؟
We left the younger children at home with their grandparents.	terakna el-atfāl el-sughār ind **jid**dehum	تركنا أصغر الأطفال في البيت مع أجدادهم.
Are these your children?	hādhoul oulādek	هل هؤلاء أولادك؟
The boy looks like his mother/father.	el-weled yish**beh** **um**ma/abooh	الولد يشبه أمه/أبوه.
The girl looks like her father/mother.	el-bint tish**beh** ab**oo**ha/**um**maha	البنت تشبه أبوها/أمها.
How old is he/she?	kem [shged] umra/**um**raha	كم عمره/عمرها.
My daughter is fourteen.	**bin**ty **um**reha arba‘**ta**‘esh sena	بنتي عمرها أربع عشرة سنة.

Vocabulary

aunt	**amma** [**khāla**]	عمة [خالة]
birthday	eed meelād	عيد ميلاد
cousin	ibn **amm** [ibn **khāl**]	إبن العم [إبن خال]
divorce	talāg	طلاق
in-laws	hima [**khawāl**]	حماة
marriage	zowāj	زواج
relatives	gerāyib	أقارب
uncle	amm [**khāl**]	عم [خال]
wedding	irs	عرس

About Homes

We have a house in town/in the country.	**in**dena bait fy el-me**dee**na/fy el-**gar**ya	عندنا بيت في المدينة/ في القرية.
We have	**in**dena	لنا
a detached two-storey house.	**men**zil bi-tābu**gain**	منزل مستقل بطابقين.
a semi-detached house.	**men**zil **mut**tesil bi-**ā**khar min **ta**ref wāhid **fa**gat	منزل متصل بآخر من ناحية واحدة فقط.
a cottage.	kookh	كوخ
a maisonette.	**sheg**ga min tābu**gain**	شقة من طابقين.
a flat.	**sheg**ga	شقة.
We have a large garden/a patio.	**in**dena ha**dee**ga ki**bee**ra/**sā**ha	لنا حديقة كبيرة/ ساحة.
There are two living rooms. One has a French window and the other a bay window.	feeha ghurfe**tain** lil-je**loos** **wā**hida liha shib**bāk** fe**ren**sy wa el-**thā**ny laha shib**bāk bā**riz min el-**hā**yit	فيه غرفتان للجلوس. وأحدة لها شباك فرنسي. والأخرى لها شباك بارز من الحائط.

There is a fireplace in the dining room.	**feeh** midf_a_ fy el-s_ā_**loun**	هناك مدفأة في الصالون.
The whole house is centrally heated.	el-**bait feeh** jih_ā_z **tedfeey**a	البيت فيه جهاز تدفئة.
The house is air conditioned.	el-bait **feeh** teh**weeya**	البيت فيه تكييف.
We have two garages.	**in**dena ger_ā_**jain**	عندنا كراجين.
The back garden has a lawn and a swimming pool.	el-had_ee_ga el-khal**feeya** feeha **makh**dhara wa **mes**bah	الحديقة الخلفية فيها مخضرة ومسبح.
In our village there are many old houses.	**in**dena fy el-**gar**ya ke**theer** min el-men_ā_zil el-ged_ee_ma	عندنا في القرية كثير من المنازل القديمة.
We prefer a modern house.	nu**fadhil** bait min el-tur_ā_z el-had_ee_th	نفضل بيت عصري.
What kind of house have you got?	**shloun** baitkum **intum**	ما نوع بيتكم؟
I like Arabic houses.	e**hibb** el-byoot el-are**beeya**	أحب البيوت العربية.
Do you cook by gas or electricity?	tatbu**khoon** ala el-**gh_ā_z** ou el-**kah**ruba	هل تطبخوا على الغاز أو الكهرباء؟
In a warm climate tiled floors are delightful.	fy el-beled el-**h_ā_r** el-bel_ā_t **ery**ah	في المناخ الحار يبدو البلاط مريح.
Wall-to-wall carpeting makes a house warm in winter.	el-**farsh** el-k_ā_mil yu**deffy** el-**bait** bil-**shi**ta	الفرش الكامل يدفء المنازل بالشتاء.
Built-in cupboards make a room seem larger.	**teb**du el-**ghur**fa muttesi'a bi-khez_ā_yin el-**h_ā_**yit	تبدو الغرفة متسعة بخزائن الحائط.
Old furniture is lovely but very expensive.	el-eth_ā_th el-ateeg je**meel** wel_ā_kin gh_ā_ly **jid**den	الأثاث العتيق جميل ولكن غال جداً.

VOCABULARY.

balcony	**bālkoun** [**shurfa**]	بلكون [شرفة]
brick	**girmeed** [**tāboog**]	قرميد
ceiling	**seguf**	سقف
chimney	**med**khena	مدخنة
door	bāb	باب
drains	**genāt** [**enābeeb**]	قناة [انابيب]
(mains) electricity	tou**seel** el-**kah**ruba el-**asly**	توصيل الكهربا الرئيسية
foundations	**esās**	أساس
gable	**wājihet** el-ja'**loun**	واجهة الجملون
gas	ghāz	غاز
plumbing	**sibāka**	سباكة
roof	**seguf**	سقف
terrace	**sa**tah	سطح
tiles	**belāt**	بلاط [زليج]
wall	**jidār** [**hāyit**]	جدار [حائط]
water	ma [**māy**, **el-ma**]	ماء
window	shib**bāk** [shib**bāch**]	شباك
window frame	i**tār** el-shib**bāk**	إطار الشباك
window pane	zu**jāj** [**jām**]	زجاج [جام]
wood	**kha**sheb	خشب

Looking After Your Money

The Bank

Where is the nearest bank?	**wain** egrab **benk**	أين أقرب بنك؟
Do you accept traveller's cheques?	tigbel shaikāt siyāheeya	هل تقبلون شيكات سياحية؟
Do you issue money against a credit card?	tidfa'oon floos mugābil kart dhimāna	هل تدفعون فلوس مقابل كارت ضمانة؟
I am expecting a remittance.	**en**tedhir hawāla māleeya an tureeg el-benk	أنني انتظر حوالة مالية عن طريق البنك.
I have a letter of credit.	indy khitāb dhimān	عندي خطاب ضمان.
I would like a draft to send away.	**wid**dy ersil hawāla māleeya	أريد أن أبعث حوالة مالية.
What is the rate of exchange for the pound/dollar/ Australian dollar?	ish si'r tah**weel** el-ji**na**ih/el-dulār/ el-dulār el-istrāly	ما سعر تحويل الجنيه/ الدولار/ الدولار الاسترالي؟
How much commission do you charge?	ish el-u**moo**la elly tākhidhoonha	ما العمولة التي تأخذونها
Please give me some change.	min **fadh**lek atny ba'edh el-**fek**ka [**khur**da]	من فضلك، أعطني بعض الفكة.
Can you split this cheque into several currencies?	**yum**kin teg**seem** el-shaik **hā**dha ila **id**det imlāt	هل يمكني تقسيم هذا الشيك إلى عدة عملات؟
I will have some Egyptian piastres/ Lebanese pounds/ Jordanian Dinar.	eby gu**roosh** masreeya/ jinaihāt libnāneeya/ denāneer erdeneeya	أحب قروش مصرية. ليرات لبنانية. ودنانير أردنية.

Can I open a temporary bank account?	**mum**kin eftah hisāb fy el-benk muweggeten	هل يمكن أن أفتح حساب في البنك مؤقتاً؟
Can you arrange for some money to be sent from my bank in Britain?	**yum**kin tahweel ba'edh el-emwāl min benky fy breetānya	هل يمكن تحويل بعض الأموال من بنكي في بريطانيا؟
I seem to be ten ... short. Can you please count it again?	el-kemmeeya nāgisa ashera ... **mum**kin tu'eed el-hisāb min **fadh**lek	الكمية ناقصة عشرة... ممكن تعيد الحساب من فضلك
Have you a card showing current exchange rates?	**in**dekum lāyihet es'ār teb**deel** el-imlāt	هل عندكم لائحة أسعار تبديل العملات؟

Vocabulary

Bank of England	benk in**gil**tera	بنك انجلترا
cashier	serrāf	صراف
cheque book	**def**ter shaikāt	دفتر الشيكات
coins	meskookāt	مسكوكات
credit	hisāb	حساب
debit	medeen	مدين
deposit slip	geseemet eedā'	قسيمة ايداع
foreign exchange regulations	guwāneen tahweel el-umla	قوانين تحويل العملة
manager	mudeer	مدير
notes	imla waregeeya	عملة ورقية
signature	tougee'	توقيع

Bureau de Change

| Are you open outside banking hours? | tifta**hoon** ghair ougāt el-benk el-ādeeya | هل تفتحون غير أوقات البنك العادية؟ |

Does the rate of exchange alter outside normal hours?	yite**gheyy**er si'r el-sarf ba'ad ou**gāt** el-dawām	هل يتغير سعر الصرف بعد اوقات الدوام؟
Are you open on Sundays?	tifta**hoon** youm el-ahed	هل تفتحون يوم الأحد؟
Can you show me your rates of exchange?	**mum**kin ti'**toon**ny si'r el-tahweel el-mou**jood** indekum	ممكن تعطوني سعر التحويل الموجود عندكم؟
Do you give the same rate for notes as for travellers' cheques?	ti'**toon** nefs el-si'r lil-ou**rāg** el-**māl**eeya wa el-shai**kāt** el-siyā**hee**ya	هل تعطون نفس السعر للأوراق المالية والشيكات السياحية؟

On Losing Traveller's Cheques or Credit Cards

When this happens you should immediately notify the company that has issued the cheques or card but you may need help from a local hotelier or banker.

I have lost my traveller's cheques/ credit card.	dhā'et minny shai**kāt** siyā**hee**ya/kart dhi**mā**na	ضاعت مني شيكات سياحية/ كارت ضمانة.
May I ask them to communicate with me through you?	**yum**kin tekoon **sil**et el-wasl **bain**na	هل يمكن أن تكونوا صلة الوصل بيننا؟
Have you a British representative?	**in**dekum mu**meth**thil ing**lai**zy	هل عندكم ممثل انجليزي؟
I hope they will be able to refund the cheques quickly. I have no other money.	**eme**ly en yu**rid**du geemet el-shaik bi**sur**'a. mā indy nu**good ukh**ra	أملي أن يردوا قيمة الشيك بسرعة. ليس لدي نقود أخرى.
I will ask my bank at home to send some money to you.	**at**lub min el-benk fy **bel**edy **yur**sil likum ba'edh el-māl	ساطلب من البنك في بلدي أن يرسل لكم بعض المال.

Will you accept a
British cheque in
payment of the hotel
bill?

tigba**loon** shai**kāt**
inglai**zee**ya mu**gā**bil
fātoo**ret** el-oo**tail**

هل تقبلون شيكات انجليزية
مقابل فاتورة الهوتيل؟

Reference Section

Numbers

1	wāhid	١
2	ithnain	٢
3	thelātha	٣
4	arbe'a	٤
5	khamsa	٥
6	sitta	٦
7	seb'a	٧
8	thimānya	٨
9	tis'a	٩
10	ashera	١٠
11	hida'esh	١١
12	ithna'esh	١٢
13	thelethta'esh	١٣
14	arba'ta'esh	١٤
15	khamsta'esh	١٥
16	sitta'esh	١٦
17	seba'ta'esh	١٧
18	thementa'esh	١٨
19	tisa'ta'esh	١٩
20	ishreen	٢٠
21	wāhid u ishreen	٢١
22	ithnain u ishreen	٢٢
23	thelātha u ishreen	٢٣
24	arbe'a u ishreen	٢٤
25	khamsa u ishreen	٢٥
26	sitta u ishreen	٢٦
27	seb'a u ishreen	٢٧
28	thimānya u ishreen	٢٨
29	tis'a u ishreen	٢٩
30	thelātheen	٣٠
40	arba'een	٤٠
50	khamseen	٥٠

60	sit**teen**	٦٠
70	seb'**een**	٧٠
80	thim**āneen**)	٨٠
90	tis'**een**	٩٠
100	m**i**ya [m**i**yet]	١٠٠
101	m**i**ya u w**ā**hid	١٠١
110	m**i**ya u ashera	١١٠
200	miy**tain**	٢٠٠
1000	elf	١٠٠٠
1001	elf u w**ā**hid	١٠٠١
2000	elf**ain**	٢٠٠٠
1,000,000	mel**youn**	١,٠٠٠,٠٠٠
1,000,000,000	elf mel**youn**	١,٠٠٠,٠٠٠,٠٠٠

first	el-**ouwel**	الأول
second	el-**thāny**	الثاني
third	el-**thālith**	الثالث
fourth	el-**rābi'**	الرابع
fifth	el-**khāmis**	الخامس
sixth	el-**sādis**	السادس
seventh	el-**sābi'**	السابع
eighth	el-**thāmin**	الثامن
ninth	el-**tāsi'**	التاسع
tenth	el-**āshir**	العاشر

once	**mar**ra	مرة
twice	marra**tain**	مرتين
three times	the**lāth** marr**āt**	ثلاث مرات

a half	nuss	نصف
a quarter	**ru**ba'	ربع
a third	thulth	ثلث
an eighth	thumn	ثمن

| a pair of | zouj min | زوج من |
| a dozen | **des**ta [douz**ee**na] | دستة [دوزينة] |

Time

It should be borne in mind that the year is measured by two different kinds of calendar in Arab countries. One of these is the Gregorian one in use throughout the western world and the other is a lunar calendar, the Hegira, which begins with Mohammed's journey from Mecca to Medina in AD 622. One of the most important months of the lunar calendar is Ramadan. During this period Muslim Arabs fast and do not drink or smoke from sunrise to sunset. After sunset food is eaten and restaurants often stay open all night. Ramadan is a religious festival and also provides an opportunity for social get-togethers of families and friends in the evenings.

Greenwich Mean Time	tougeet greenich	توقيت غرينتش.
Date line	tougeet	توقيت.
am/pm	gabl el-**dhu**her/ba'd el-**dhu**her	قبل الظهر/ بعد الظهر. [ق . ظ] [ب . ظ]
24 hour clock	tougeet bi-**ar**ba' wa 'ish**reen** sā'a	التوقيت بأربع وعشرين ساعة.
summertime	tougeet el-saif	توقيت الصيف.
It is	el-sā'a	الساعة
12.15	the**na**'esh u **ru**ba'	الثانية عشرة والربع
12.20	the**na**'esh u ish**reen** de**gee**ga	الثانية عشرة وثلث
12.30	the**na**'esh u nuss	الثانية عشرة ونصف
12.35	the**na**'esh u**kham**sa u the**lā**theen	الثانية عشر ونصف وخمسة
12.45	**wā**hid illa **ru**ba'	واحدة إلا الربع
1.00	el-**wā**hid	الواحدة
Midnight	**mun**tasif el-lail	منتصف الليل
Midday	el-**dhu**her	الظهر

Phrases Referring to Time

What time is it?	kem el-**sā**‘a [el-**sā**‘a baish]	الساعة كم؟
It is late.	mit‘**ekh**khir	متأخرا.
It is early.	mub**ek**kir	مبكر.
Are we on time?	wu**si**lna bil-**mou**‘id	هل وصلنا في الميعاد المحدد؟
At what time shall we meet?	**mi**ta **nil**tigy	متى نلتقي؟
At what time are we expected?	**mi**ta el-**mou**‘id	متى نجيء؟
Day by day.	**youm** al-**youm**	يوما بيوم.
Every second.	kill **thā**nya	كل ثانية.
At regular intervals.	bi fet**rāt** mu‘**eyy**ena	في أوقات منتظمة
After the clock strikes.	**lem**man te**digg** el-**sā**‘a	بعد أن تدق الساعة.
days	ey**yām**	أيام
weeks	e**sābee**‘	أسابيع
years	sene**wāt**	سنوات
Sunday	el-**ahed**	الأحد
Monday	el-ith**nain**	الاثنين
Tuesday	el-the**lātha**	الثلاثاء
Wednesday	el-**arbi**‘a	الأربعاء
Thursday	el-khe**mees**	الخميس
Friday	el-**jum**‘a	الجمعة
Saturday	el-**sebt**	السبت
daybreak	**shegg**it el-**nour**	فجر [في مطلع النهار]
dawn	**fi**jer	فجر

morning	sabāh	صباح
afternoon	ba'd el-**dh**uher	الظهر
evening	**me**sa	مساء
night	lail	ليل
today	el-youm	اليوم
yesterday	ems	أمس
tomorrow	**buk**ra [**bā**chir]	غدا
the day before yesterday	ouwel**tems**	اليوم قبل الأمس
two days ago	**ga**bul you**main**	قبل يومين
the day after tomorrow	ba'ad **buk**ra [ugub **bā**chir]	اليوم بعد غدا
the following day	**tā**ly youm	اليوم التالي
weekday	**you**min fy wast el-us**boo'**	يوم في وسط الأسبوع
a day off	youm i**jā**za	يوم إجازة
birthday	eed mee**lād**	عيد ميلاد
Christmas Day	eed mee**lād** el-me**seeh**	يوم عيد ميلاد المسيح
New Year's Day	rās el-**se**na [dourt el-**se**na]	يوم رأس السنة
All Saints' Day	eed kull el-giddee**seen**	عيد كل القديسين
May Day	**ou**wel **mā**yu	أول مايو
weekend	**ut**let ākhir el-us**boo'**	عطلة آخر الأسبوع
last week	el-us**boo'** el-**mā**dhy	الأسبوع الماضي
next week	el-us**boo'** el-**gā**dim	الأسبوع القادم
for two weeks	**mud**det usboo'**ain**	لمدة أسبوعين
January	ye**nā**yir	يناير
February	feb**rā**yir	فبراير
March	**mā**ris	مارس

April	ibreel	أبريل
May	māyu	مايو
June	yoonyu	يونيو
July	yoolyu	يوليو
August	aghustus	أغسطس
September	sibtember	سبتمبر
October	uktoober	اكتوبر
November	noofember	نوفمبر
December	deesember	ديسمبر
calendar month	shaher shemsy	شهر شمسي
lunar month	shaher gamery	شهر قمري
monthly	shahry	شهري
since January	mundhu shaher yenāyir	منذ شهر يناير
last month	el-shaher el-mādhy	الشهر الماضي
next month	el-shaher el-gādim	الشهر القادم
the month before	el-shaher el-sābig	الشهر السابق
the first of March	owwel māris	أول مارس
Spring	rebee'	ربيع
Summer	saif	صيف
Autumn	khereef	خريف
Winter	shita	شتاء
years	sineen	سنين
BC/AD	gabl el-meelād/ba'ed el-meelād	قبل الميلاد / بعد الميلاد

Temperature Equivalents

FAHRENHEIT		CENTIGRADE
212	Boiling point	100
100		37·8
98·4	Body temperature	37
86		30
77		25
68		20
50		10
32	Freezing point	0
0		−17·8

To convert Fahrenheit to Centigrade subtract 32 and divide by 1·8.

To convert Centigrade to Fahrenheit multiply by 1·8 and add 32.

Pressure

The barometer tells you the air pressure of the atmosphere: 15 lb. per sq. in. is normal air pressure at sea level. This equals 1·06 kg. per sq. cm.

A tyre gauge tells you the pressure of your car tyres.

POUNDS PER SQUARE INCH	KILOGRAMS PER SQUARE CENTIMETRE
16	1·12
18	1·27
20	1·41
22	1·55
24	1·69
26	1·83
28	1·97

Measurement of Distance

One kilometre = 1000 metres = 0·62 miles.

One hundred centimetres = 1 metre = 3·28 ft.

One centimetre = 0·39 inches.

The following table gives equivalents for metres and feet. The figure in the centre column can stand for either feet or metres and the equivalent should then be read off in the appropriate column.

METRES	METRES AND FEET	FEET
0·30	1	3·28
0·61	2	6·56
0·91	3	9·84
1·22	4	13·12
1·52	5	16·40
1·83	6	19·69
2·13	7	22·97
2·44	8	26·25
2·74	9	29·53
3·05	10	32·81
3·35	11	36·09
3·66	12	39·37
3·96	13	42·65
4·27	14	45·93
4·57	15	49·21
4·88	16	52·49
5·18	17	55·77
5·49	18	59·06
5·79	19	62·34
6·10	20	65·62
7·62	25	82·02
15·24	50	164·04
22·86	75	264·06
30·48	100	328·08

MILES	MILES AND KILOMETRES	KILOMETRES
0·62	1	1·61
1·24	2	3·22
1·86	3	4·82
2·49	4	6·44
3·11	5	8·05
3·73	6	9·66
4·35	7	11·27
4·97	8	12·88
5·59	9	14·48
6·21	10	16·09
15·53	25	40·23
31·07	50	80·47
46·60	75	120·70
62·14	100	160·93

For motorists it is useful to remember that

30 miles is 48·3 km.   70 miles is 112·7 km.

but

70 km. is 43·5 miles   100 km. is 62·1 miles

To convert kilometres to miles, divide by 8 and multiply by 5.

To convert miles to kilometres, divide by 5 and multiply by 8.

Measurements of Quantity

Weight

POUNDS	POUNDS AND KILOGRAMS	KILOGRAMS
2·21	1	0·45
4·41	2	0·91
6·61	3	1·36
8·82	4	1·81
11·02	5	2·27

POUNDS	POUNDS AND KILOGRAMS		KILOGRAMS
13·23	6		2·72
15·43	7		3·18
17·64	8		3·63

OUNCES	GRAMS	OUNCES	GRAMS
0·5	14·18	6	170·10
1	28·35	7	198·45
2	56·70	8 (½ lb.)	226·80
3	85·05	12	340·19
4	113·40	16 (1 lb.)	453·59
5	141·75		

One kilogram = 1000 grams = 2·2 lb.
Half a kilogram = 500 grams = 1·1 lb.
When shopping for small items, it is useful to remember that
   100 grams is about 3½ oz.
One metric ton is 1000 kilograms.

Liquid Measures

U.K. PINTS	U.K. PINTS AND LITRES	LITRES
1·76	1	0·57
3·52	2 (1 quart)	1·14
5·28	3	1·70
7·04	4	2·27
8·80	5	2·84
10·56	6	3·41
12·32	7	3·98
14·08	8 (1 gallon)	4·55
15·84	9	5·11
17·60	10	5·68

1 litre = 1·76 pints.
One tenth of a litre is a decilitre or 0·18 of a pint.
One hundredth of a litre is a centilitre or 0·018 of a pint.
One hundred litres are a hectolitre or 22 gallons.
One gallon = 4·55 litres.
One quart = 1·14 litres.
One pint = 0·57 litres.

Clothing Sizes

Measurements for clothes are made according to the metric system in Arabic-speaking countries. Here are the equivalent sizes for the main articles of clothing:

Women

DRESSES AND COATS

Britain	34	36	38	40	42	44	46
United States	32	34	36	38	40	42	44
Middle East	40	42	44	46	48	50	52

Men

SUITS

Britain and United States	36	38	40	42	44	46
Middle East	46	48	50	52	54	56

SHIRTS

Britain and United States	14	14½	15	15½	16	16½	17
Middle East	36	37	38	39	41	42	43

Index to Phrases